# What is Brand Equity, Anyway?

LEO iQ

*Selected papers on brands and advertising by*
## Paul Feldwick

'What is the answer to the question being asked in cocktail lounges, all the time, all over America – "What is brand equity, anyway, and how do you measure it?"'

Thornton C. Lockwood

**World Advertising Research Center**

First published 2002

World Advertising Research Center
Farm Road, Henley-on-Thames
Oxfordshire RG9 1EJ, United Kingdom
Telephone: +44 (0) 1491 411000
Facsimile: +44 (0) 1491 418600
E-mail: enquiries@warc.com

Copyright © World Advertising Research Center 2002

A CIP catalogue record for this book is
available from the British Library

ISBN 1 84116 109 8

Typeset in 10/13pt Palatino by Marie Doherty
Printed and bound in Great Britain by Page Brothers (Norwich) Ltd,
Norwich, Norfolk NR6 6SA

'This is a wonderful book. Paul is a thought leader who makes the rest of us think a great deal better.'

Tim Ambler, London Business School

'This collection of Paul's papers is the distillation of wide reading, practical experience and deep reflection. It covers the key issues which advertising researchers – and behind them advertisers and ad agencies – worry about today.'

Simon Broadbent, BrandCon

'In probing the layers of fat that have slowly accumulated around the idea of brand equity he has made many other overweight concepts considerably lighter. Ideas such as brand, brand loyalty, brand strength, brand value, brand image, brand personality and brand salience suddenly become clear.'

Wendy Gordon, The Fourth Room

'This succinct and well-written volume discusses brands in the round and also the role of advertising.'

Professor John Philip Jones, University of Syracuse, New York

'What a pleasure it is to read a book on the business of marketing which is not guilty of either of the modern evils of self-serving bias or comparative illiteracy!'

Mike Sommers, Chief Marketing Officer, Royal and Sun Alliance

# Contents

# Introduction:
# Questions of Measurement

We talk about *strong* brands, *successful* campaigns, *powerful* ads, but how can we measure the 'strength' of a brand, the 'power' of an advertising execution, the 'success' of an advertising campaign?

These are not innocent or academic questions. The old management adage that 'what gets measured, gets done' applies to this field as to any other, so choosing the wrong metrics for any of these may be dangerous – as dangerous as choosing to use no metrics at all (which is often, in practice, the easiest way out).

The eight papers collected in this volume deal in various ways with these questions. I wrote them as separate pieces between 1991 and 1999, and each was designed to be read independently. Nevertheless, I hope that, when read together, they add up to something more than the sum of their parts.

The contents of this book fall into two parts. The first part focuses on *brands* and the second part on *advertising* – though this is a slightly artificial distinction, as brands and advertising are largely two sides of the same coin.

The section on brands principally addresses the question 'What is brand equity, anyway, and how do you measure it?' This was the original title of a paper I first gave at the Market Research Society Conference in 1996, and which forms the present Chapter 3. I wrote this paper because I found myself confused about what this much-used expression, brand equity, really meant. It seemed to me that people were using the term in some quite different senses; also, more dangerously, that they sometimes assumed these different senses were essentially the same. In working this through I came to the conclusion that there were three fundamentally different senses of 'brand equity', and that each of these in turn could be more closely defined and, where possible, measured in a multiplicity of ways.

When I revised this paper for the *Journal of Brand Management*, I ended it with a provocative suggestion that we would all manage as well, and perhaps better, if the words 'brand equity' were to be banned altogether. I slightly regret this now – not just because my suggestion was totally ignored, but because some people seemed to deduce from it that I was a total 'brand equity sceptic', which I'm not.

In order to put this 'brand equity' chapter into context, therefore, I preface it here with two earlier papers. I hope these make it very clear that when I criticised the *expression* 'brand equity', I in no way meant to underestimate the importance of *brands* themselves.

Chapter 1 is a general answer to that still popular question, 'What is a brand?'. It was originally written for the Account Planning Group's valuable book, *Understanding Brands*. Chapter 2 was co-written with my colleague from Paris, Françoise Bonnal, in response to a journalistic craze of the early 1990s – the dramatic claim that brands were dead. This may all seem like water under the bridge today. Indeed, it is hard to believe that authoritative commentators such as the *Wall Street Journal* went overboard on such a dubious theory. However, I believe it bears reprinting now in order to emphasise that brands are not a transient phenomenon. (It may also come in useful the next time the 'death of brands' story comes around. I predict that next time it appears it will be dressed up with some new variations, among which 'anti-globalisation' will be one prominent theme.)

While I was gratified by the amount of interest which the 'brand equity' paper aroused, I did feel that I may have taken the easy route – that is, of criticising everyone else's proposals for how to measure brand strength without being at all clear as to what ought to be done in practice. I was therefore pleased when, a couple of years later, Colin McDonald and Phyllis Vangelder invited me to write the chapter on brand research for the new *ESOMAR Handbook of Market and Opinion Research*. This is now Chapter 4. I know this still doesn't give any easy answers – I do not know of any that I believe in – but I do hope it provides a more positive and constructive review of the various techniques for measuring the different senses of 'brand equity'.

In the second half of the book, the focus shifts from measurement of *brand* strength to measurement of *advertising* strength. Chapter 5, originally a paper in *Admap*, begins by putting this often stormy area into some organisational context. Advertising research might be easier if it could be treated as a disinterested quest for truth, devoid of passion and politics – but it is not, so perhaps we should face up to the fact before going on to Chapter 6, which is a (fairly) dispassionate review of copy-testing methods and philosophies. Then Chapter 7, written for the Account Planning Group's book *How to Plan Advertising*, offers a practical summary of key issues and techniques in evaluating ad campaigns once they have been exposed in the marketplace.

The final chapter, which has not been published before, was given as a paper at one of Mike Sainsbury's ASI conferences in Prague. It offers a different kind of commentary on the subject of this book, by examining the history of how practitioners and researchers have thought about advertising. Is advertising a science, with effects that can be measured and rules and regularities that can be deduced from observation? Or is it an art, which continually redefines rules and defies measurement? This debate, as the chapter shows, has been going on for at least a hundred years (in a slightly different form, perhaps, since the time of Plato and Aristotle). The discussion points forward to a bigger question, which is not directly addressed but continually casts its shadow over all these pieces – 'how does advertising work?'. That, however, must be material for another book.

In editing these pieces for republication, I have taken the opportunity to make them, I hope, a bit more readable. I have not, however, otherwise attempted to rewrite or update them, because I would have ended up wanting to create a new book altogether. There is a certain amount of overlap or repetition between them as easily happens with reprinted papers, especially between chapters 3 and 4. I think removing this would have made the book harder to read, rather than easier, so I hope it is not too irritating.

Many people have, consciously or not, contributed to the contents of this book – some through their constructive criticism of individual papers, some by inviting and encouraging me to write them in the first place, and some more generally in discussion and debate. These include Tim Ambler, Chris Baker, Patrick Barwise, Françoise Bonnal, Simon Broadbent, Gordon Brown, Linda Caller, the late Charles Channon, Alan Cooper, Don Cowley, Jim Crimmins, Leslie de Chernatony, Andrew Ehrenberg, Wendy Gordon, David Haigh, Robert Heath, David Jenkins, John Philip Jones, Colin McDonald, Gil McWilliam, Mike Sainsbury, the late Nicholas Staveley, Phyllis Vangelder, Rosi Ware, and Roderick White, with thanks and apologies to those others I may have inadvertently left out and to all those colleagues and friends from whom I have learned whatever I know. None of these people will necessarily agree with anything I have written here, and the opinions and errors are, of course, all mine. I am also grateful to the management of BMP DDB for making it possible for me to write and research these pieces; to Raquel Suárez of DDB University and to Richard Morris and Glen Lomas of BMP DDB for their support; and to Mike Waterson and his colleagues at the World Advertising Research Center for making this book a reality. Lastly I am much indebted to the original publishers of these articles for their permission to reprint them here, and full acknowledgements to each of them appear at the beginning of each chapter.

Paul Feldwick
December 2001

Part One

# On Brands

# Chapter 1
# What is a Brand?

## Introduction

Towards the end of 1989 the Marketing Society held a major conference in London. Its title was 'The Immortal Brand', and its publicity made prominent use of a quote from the Group Chief Executive of United Biscuits:

'Buildings age and become dilapidated.
Machines wear out.
People die.
But what live on are the brands.'

The visual design accompanying this theme was striking. The immortal brand was represented by a stylised, golden sun with a face on, reminiscent of an entertainment at the court of *le roi soleil*. The sun rose above a classical montage of Greek temples, broken columns and Herculean statues. The metaphor was clear: the brand as deity, a sentient being whose existence transcends our merely human lifespan.

And indeed, this is how we in marketing and advertising talk of brands. They have life cycles; they have personalities. In our research we personify brands, and find consumers can play the game. Unconsciously we credit the brand with some kind of absolute, platonic existence. Our mission is to *discover* (rather than invent) its 'core values' and abide by them. In fact, the brand is a rather primitive kind of god. If we keep its laws and regularly pay the tributes due (such as advertising), fortune will smile on us – otherwise, disaster.

Originally published as 'Defining a brand', in *Understanding Brands* (D. Cowley, ed.). Copyright © Paul Feldwick, 1991, published by Kogan Page. Permission for using this material has been granted by the publisher.

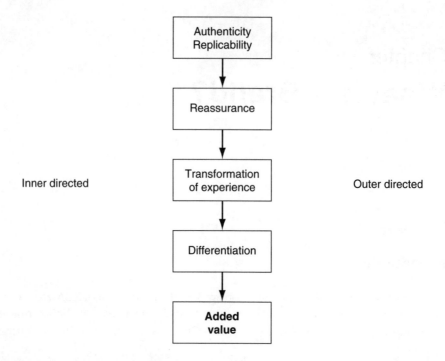

**Figure 1.1**   Sources of added value in branding.

Now most of this is a way of saying valuable and important things about branding. Brands can 'live' longer than people. The metaphor of personality has been helpful, and I shall use it myself later. But it may be worthwhile at the start of this book to remind ourselves that it *is* only a metaphor. A brand may have 'personality', but it is not a person, still less a god on a cloud. You cannot talk to it, and it cannot answer you back. In fact, a brand has no absolute or objective existence – nor are its 'core values' written on a tablet of stone in the Gobi Desert. A brand is simply a collection of perceptions in the mind of the consumer (Figure 1.1).

What I want to do in this chapter is to start from the consumer. Why does this phenomenon called branding – about which we get so mystical – exist at all? Presumably it satisfies certain needs on the part of the consumer: but what are they? How does branding work, and under what conditions?

The tentative answers in this chapter – and I regard it as only a viewpoint which I hope others may improve on – are rather complex. Branding can be seen as satisfying various different needs, and working at different levels and in different ways. What I will suggest has happened is that brands begin as a badge or promise of certainty in an uncertain world, and that this offers simple and functional benefits to any consumer. However, because a brand offers this sort of certainty, it also becomes a type of currency for consumers to carry out less obviously related kinds of transactions with themselves and with each other. In a sense, consumers have 'hijacked' brands for their own purposes, but all the ways in which brands can be used derive from the basic promise of certainty, and I will therefore argue that we are talking about one coherent, if complex phenomenon. Brands as a badge, and brands as personality are aspects of the same thing.

At its simplest, a brand is a recognisable and trustworthy badge of origin, and also a promise of performance.

## A badge of origin

All histories of marketing or advertising refer to the Bass Red Triangle, registered as the first trade mark in England in 1876 and (I am glad to say) still going strong. It will serve as a good example of branding at its simplest – as a guarantee of authenticity.

This is something we rather take for granted, but it is of fundamental importance in underpinning the mechanisms of branding. When we buy a jar of Hellmann's mayonnaise, we can be fairly sure it *is* a jar of Hellmann's mayonnaise. Rigorous legislation in this country prevents forgery or 'passing off'. When this was less true than today, many packaging designs were as elaborate as banknotes, to discourage forgery and emphasise authenticity ('None genuine without this signature'). Once this confidence is breached, the symbols, and hence the satisfaction of a brand, lose their potency. (How am I to recognise a *real* Lacoste sports shirt nowadays?)

Many of the higher-value satisfactions of brands depend crucially on this belief in authenticity. This point will be particularly stressed in the later section on transformation of experience. In the meantime, just consider this: a fake Rolex watch may fool everyone else, but *it won't fool you*.

## The promise of performance

The other reason that we believe in brands is because, on the whole, they keep their promises. If every bottle of Heinz tomato ketchup tasted different from the last, the brand would have little meaning. If consumers are prepared to forgive an exceptional bad experience from a trusted brand, this is because they know it is exceptional. On a familiar product the brand name offers a replicable degree, and kind, of customer satisfaction.

The product itself need not remain, literally, unchanged. Certain products, such as newspapers, change constantly by their very nature. Most successful brands continually improve or update their products to remain competitive, or to meet changed market requirements. However, if the product does not reliably live up to the promise, the brand, however strong its history, eventually loses its force. Coca-Cola, one of the world's best-loved brands, provoked howls of betrayal with its ill-judged reformulation of 'New Coke'. Even in a market where we tend to think of 'image' transcending product reality, the poor quality of Jaguar cars which were built in the early 1970s did great damage to the marque's reputation, which was repaired with difficulty. Even a gradual decline in product performance can have the same effect, as when Cadbury's reduced the thickness of their Dairy Milk chocolate bar by imperceptible stages, until it was competitively vulnerable to the launch of Rowntree's Yorkie.

At best, a strong brand may provide a time-lag between the product becoming uncompetitive, and consumer rejection of it. In the early 1970s users of Cadbury's Smash remained loyal to the brand of instant mashed potato, despite the launch of a technically superior product from Wondermash. This provided a breathing space for Cadbury's in which to match the new formulation, but it is unlikely that it would have survived for ever with the inferior product. Sooner or later, failure to deliver renders a brand meaningless.

The extent to which product delivery ultimately underlies the strength of brands is often forgotten by those who subscribe to the myth of 'the brand in the sky'. Sooner or later, product realities will rewrite reputations, however powerful they are.

At this stage the benefits to the consumer are clear. The brand offers a strong promise of both *authenticity* and *replicability*. Indeed without these, consumer decision-making would become a lottery and, probably, a nightmare. The promise, however, is more than an aid to decision-making. A promise actually creates value in its own right, by enhancing the experience of owning or using the product.

## The value of reassurance

Consider the satisfactions of owning a motor car. Many of these are tangible experiences: the comfort of the seats; the pleasure of driving it; its added comforts, such as air-conditioning or a stereo; its beauty to the eye; its speed and performance, for those who like that sort of thing...

However, there are other requirements from a car which are less tangible. It is important, for example, that the car will not break down. The fact that it hasn't done so in the past is real; the expectation that it won't do so in the future is hypothetical. The degree of reassurance I personally feel as to whether the car will break down, when starting my journey, makes a major difference to my satisfaction as a user of the car. Branding can make a major difference to that reassurance. What the brand name does is translate a very hypothetical, negative kind of product superiority, into a real and immediate experience. I set out confident, relaxed, able to enjoy the trip. The value that I place on this feeling is part of the value that I may be prepared to pay for the brand, over and above the value I perceive in the nuts and bolts of the visible car. (For years, Volkswagen advertising in the UK was founded on the brand's *reliability*: as a result the marque commanded a significant price premium over comparable cars in its class.)

This is one example, but it is generally applicable to many other and less obvious situations. The reassurance I derive from the brand name (of performance, of authenticity) actually enhances the value I derive from the use of the product, over and above the physical evidence of my senses. While buying, cooking or serving my preferred brand of baked beans, I derive a heightened pleasure of anticipation long before I taste them. If serving drinks to guests, I am confident that a certain brand will be enjoyed by them, which puts me at my ease. If wearing clothes bearing the label of a famous designer, I feel more confident that they will look good under all circumstances – even if I lack confidence in my own judgement of style. In every case the added value consists in the fact that I can relax and enjoy the experience, confident that the brand *promises* that all problems are taken care of.

## Transformation of experience

What we have discovered here is that the subjective experience of using a *brand* can be different from the subjective experience of using an identical product without the brand reassurance. At one level, you could say this is just a matter of paying for peace of mind – not that we should underestimate this, but there's more to it. There is evidence that beliefs about the brand can actually affect perceptions of the physical product characteristics.

The simplest example is of the blind vs. branded product test. It can very commonly be shown that consumers tasting two food or drink brands comparatively may express a clear preference for one over the other (often the one with the greater market share), while the same product test conducted blind shows no clear preference. Branding, in short, *transforms* the actual experience of using the product – and thereby adds to its value.

One of the most striking demonstrations of the real value to the consumer of the brand experience was found in the analgesics market, as reported in the *British Medical Journal* (Branthwaite & Cooper, 1981). Patients taking their own preferred brand of analgesic (as opposed to a chemically identical own-label product) claimed faster relief from pain. Doctors recognise this as the *placebo* effect, and it demonstrates that certain symptoms respond to the *ritual* of taking medicine as much as to the physical substance. The blind vs. branded product test demonstrates that this principle is applicable in many other circumstances.

The idea of transformation is a very powerful one, and reflects the way in which much advertising and branding works. In 1987 many people's imaginations were gripped by the story of the Nanking Cargo, a load of porcelain sunk for 200 years in the South China Sea. The items themselves are no different from much other porcelain already available, but the experience of owning or handling one of these bowls is rendered quite different by the knowledge of its extraordinary and romantic history. As a result such dishes sell for a considerable premium, the added value for which collectors will pay. The parallel with a commercial 'brand' is clear: both hinge on the *authenticity* of the goods.

It is commonly asserted that paying more 'for the name' is a foolish delusion on the part of the customer, and little more than a confidence trick on the part of the seller. Yet the benefit to the customer is a real enhancement of his experience of consumption, whether it consists in peace of mind or an imaginative experience.

To understand this we need to understand that the benefits sought by most consumers are subjective, and go a stage or two beyond the product's literal function. Charles Revlon used to say that others sold cosmetics, he sold *hope*. Parallel benefits can be imagined for any other type of product. People who buy toothpaste actually want *confidence* and *security* – that their teeth won't fall out, that their breath won't smell. People who buy tennis rackets or golf balls are buying the belief that they can win. A mother buying detergent is buying a way of presenting and showing affection for her family. Children selecting breakfast cereals are choosing *fun*... and so on. What is really on sale is an abstraction – and in all these cases, it will come from the brand, rather than the product. (Frequently, as the blind vs. branded tests show, the benefits are *projected* back on to the product itself.)

## Differentiation and 'brand personality'

Thus the transformation that takes place is not merely an intensification of the experience, but an import of ideas which translate the simple function of the product into a relevant emotional metaphor. It is in this way that brand differentiation and the idea of a brand 'personality' are created. If Persil is about 'caring', it evokes at one and the same time both the perceived effect of the powder on the clothes (gentle and effective) and also the kind of emotions a mother may have about her family while washing their clothes (contrary to what cynics may think, such emotions are not entirely an adman's myth). In this way the experience of washing with Persil is qualitatively different from using, say, Ariel, and satisfies a different (perhaps a complementary) set of emotional needs from the process. Washing clothes is not after all simply a functional act; it is part of a social context of relationships both within the family, and between the family and the world outside, and this creates needs beyond the merely functional.

In further work done by Peter Cooper on the analgesics market, the enhanced effectiveness of certain brands on individuals could be related to the specific characteristics of how the brand was perceived to work. These were expressed through a role-playing exercise in which, for example, one brand behaved as soothing the pain away gently, the other as a powerful force attacking it.

It is when we enter this realm of differentiation that the metaphor of brand personality becomes extremely valuable, but it all develops naturally from the idea of consistency and familiarity. In dealing with people, 'personality' describes the ways in which we anticipate an individual will behave in particular circumstances. Of course, no one is totally predictable: but on the whole, people are predictable enough for human relationships to depend largely on this construct. Thus we create our friends, our acquaintances, and our enemies. The same is true of brands.

Consumers, as has long been recognised, can easily be encouraged to talk about brands in terms of human analogy – a technique still widely used, both qualitatively and quantitatively. What this really means is that consumers feel different relationships to different brands, depending on the type of subjective needs which the brands do or don't satisfy. Sometimes different brands appeal to different personality types; sometimes they fulfil complementary needs for the same person. In this way functionally similar products can remain competitive on grounds other than simple price.

To sum up our argument so far: a brand is fundamentally a promise, rendered credible by law and by experience. At one level this simply makes the decision process easier; at a higher level it can actually add to consumers' beneficial experience of a product, thus creating a value for which people may be prepared to pay.

The way in which the experience is transformed can be very particular to the brand, thus creating differentiation between similar products and the metaphor of personality.

## The social dimension

So far, we have (deliberately) talked as if the individual consumer and the brand manufacturer were the only two parties involved in this process. This has made the story simpler, but it is of course never true. Everything we have described so far has an added *social* dimension. An attitude towards a certain behaviour is not simply determined by my own beliefs or experiences, but also by what I imagine other (relevant) people might think of the same thing (Tuck, 1976). Our discussion of the satisfactions of owning a motor car was noticeably incomplete, because this element was left out. It may be helpful to take up this example again, in order to explore the various ways in which our decisions and perceptions can be affected by what we think other people think.

First there is a need for reassurance. Few people, in most situations, are prepared to trust their own judgement totally in isolation, without some reference to what others in the same situation believe (those few probably have a tendency to become either millionaires or bankrupts). In a complex and high-investment decision such as choosing a car, buyers characteristically make this need overt by soliciting advice in the office or pub, and by buying car magazines. Ultimately, they will often find their choice assisted by the thought that the huge numbers of people like themselves buying Fords or Vauxhalls can't be wrong. In many markets this feeling of safety in numbers contributes to the reputation of the brand leader, and has often been exploited in advertising ('a million housewives every day…', etc.).

However, this is not in itself the most important way in which others become involved in my purchase decisions. Patterns of consumption are not just driven by functional benefits – they are social statements which continually define or redefine our relationship with others, our position in society. This is true in all kinds of human society, by no means only those in which brands exist. Anthropologists have shown how in certain tribal cultures the ownership, production, giving and consumption of certain types of food define social relationships (Douglas, 1982). I have basic functional needs (to eat, to keep warm), but what and how I eat, and what I wear are partly conditioned by what society deems appropriate (to my power, status, life-stage) and partly by what kind of role I wish to assume for myself. In the case of a car purchase, this creates strong pressures which may conflict with each other, and indeed with some of the functional criteria, for a choice. All this would still hold true independent of brands: but brands are one of the key ways of defining and codifying the world, and so become an important part of the language in which these social statements are expressed. Because brands are authenticated, they become particularly robust currency for social exchange. Patterns of relative affluence, of peer group endorsement, of conformity or non-conformity, create strong social meaning for BMW vs. Mercedes, Volkswagen vs. Peugeot.

The social power of brands can be at its most overt in communal rituals of consumption – such as beer drinking. Heavy drinkers of lager tend to be young working-class males, for whom the evening's 'session' is a highly structured event with strong pressure to conform. In this context a brand of lager needs to be accepted by the group before it is OK to order it. Hofmeister, as an unknown brand, was unacceptable until George the Bear (an aspirational, surrogate group leader sharing in the group's sense of humour) positioned it.

It might also be important for the young lager drinker to be wearing the right clothes. Clothes are one of the most obvious social signs of conformity or non-conformity with a particular group, a phenomenon which of course exists separately from brands. In some contexts it might be a sufficient symbol to wear jeans; in others it might be necessary to wear a certain brand of jeans, particularly now that jeans are acceptable among a wide range of social groups and situations. Branding adds an extra level of clarity and complexity to the social language of clothes. Obvious parallels exist in many other markets: cigarettes, watches, shoes, and even household durables. (Why *does* your fridge have its name on the front?)

It is important to stress that the outer-directed value of a brand (as a badge to others) and the inner-directed value of the brand (as transformation of the user's experience) are not distinct from each other. They continually overlap, interact, and in some cases may even be different ways of looking at the same thing. Most designer labels, after all, are *inside* the clothes, not outside. A tie says 'Pierre Balmain', or 'Yves St Laurent' on the back, not the front. Realistically, most people will never see it or know what endorsement it carries, but because you feel you know what they would think of it *if they did*, you have the same (inner-directed) confidence or sense of style that comes from the name. The satisfaction of owning a particular make of car and knowing that it is socially regarded as a symbol of a certain kind of success can exist without reference to any other people actually being involved – 'it will remind you that your life has not been totally without success', as a famous ad for Jaguar once put it. Is this inner-directed or outer-directed? And does it matter? The social dimension is so pervasive in branding that it is hard to separate it out, and probably a fruitless exercise to do so.

## Conclusions

If I had to venture a one-line definition of branding, perhaps to sum up what may have seemed like an over-complex analysis, it would be to do with 'the intangible values created by a badge of reassurance'. The intangible values may be simple (peace of mind, structuring choice) or increasingly complex (gaining the approval or approbation of others, or actually defining the experience of the product itself). In the majority of cases – possibly in all cases – the satisfactions of branding are potentially a combination of these, in varying proportions. Some recent authors have suggested that brands can be classified into those which are simple, non-emotional badges of product quality, and those which offer rich emotional or symbolic values (McWilliam & de Chernatony, 1989). This has a degree of truth in so far as some brand choices involve an important rational component related to product characteristics (e.g. garden tools), while others are more obviously concerned with differentiating essentially similar products (say, cigarettes). However, this may be an over-simplistic view, which ignores the intangible, often emotional benefits that branding confers on superficially 'functional' product choices – and also overlooks the fact that emotional or socially symbolic brand values are generally based on some genuine (if perhaps historic) product qualities.

An example may illustrate the first of these points. You might consider paint to be a very functional product, where the brand name simply stands for a particular chemical composition, and qualities of covering power, durability, etc. Yet when people paint they do far more, usually, than simply cover their walls. First, they derive a powerful sense of transformation and renewal from the decorating process – brand values of a less tangible sort, 'freshness', 'naturalness' become potentially important. Second, if they apply the paint themselves (the most usual procedure) there is a strong sense of pride and achievement in 'doing the job properly' – and part of this is the choice of the 'right' brand of paint. To be seen as 'the one experts use' can be a powerful discriminator. This is, of course, underpinned by consistent product quality, but nuances of covering power or durability (which is a promise for the future anyway) are in themselves of secondary importance. By consistently making use of ideas like these in advertising, Dulux has for many years dominated the UK paint market. It may remind us that even in apparently very functional markets (washing-up liquid, kitchen towels, bathroom cleaners, etc.), product performance is still a very subjective matter.

Even in industrial purchasing decisions, which we might imagine to be completely 'rational', difficult or complex choices are likely to be referred to beliefs about the suppliers' reputation – or quite likely influenced by the perceptions of other relevant managers. 'No one ever got fired for buying IBM' ran a famous slogan. The mechanics of branding are essentially the same here as anywhere.

Branding begins by satisfying a basic human need for control and reassurance. Because it offers consistency in an otherwise uncertain world, the brand then has the potential to become a tool for dividing up the world, and a medium of social exchange. In offering reassurance and in creating rituals of consumption, branding always creates value to the consumer *beyond* the merely functional.

## References

Branthwaite, A. & Cooper, P. (1981) Analgesic effects of branding in treatment of headaches. *British Medical Journal* 282.

Douglas, M. (1982) *In The Active Voice*. Routledge and Kegan, London.

McWilliam, G. & de Chernatony, L. (1989) Representational brands and functional brands: the strategic implications of the difference. *Admap*, March, pp. 38–41.

Tuck, M. (1976) *How Do We Choose?* Methuen, London.

# Chapter 2
# Are Brands Dead?

## Introduction

Around the middle of 1993, a rash of headlines such as the following created alarm and despondency in marketing departments and advertising agencies:

'Can the big brands survive?'

*(Investors Chronicle*, 10 September 1993)

'Shoot out at the checkout – From Marlboro to Kellogg's, big brands are under siege from supermarkets' own labels. Many brands will perish or never be so profitable again.'

*(The Economist*, 5 June 1993)

'Are brand names being pushed off the shelf? – Smart prices not smart labels are increasingly the selling point in the nineties.'

*(The Guardian*, 12 June 1993)

'Is it the end of the road for brands?'

*(Media International*, September 1993)

'Survey reveals fall in brand loyalty.'

*(Marketing*, 8 July 1993)

This paper co-authored with Françoise Bonnal. Originally published as 'Reports of the death of brands have been greatly exaggerated', in *Marketing and Research Today*, 1995, 23(2), pp. 86–95.
Copyright © ESOMAR® 2001.
Permission for using this material has been granted by ESOMAR®, Amsterdam, the Netherlands.
For further information, please refer to the ESOMAR website: www.esomar.nl.

'Brands on the Run – Household names are under threat from deep discounting and the proliferation of own label products.'

(*The Observer*, 25 July 1993)

'Brands – Who needs them?'

(*The Times*, 11 August 1993)

In most cases, the articles themselves were rather more balanced and less sensational than the headlines, but the residual impression was that perhaps we were seeing some fundamental shift in the laws of marketing – that the very concept of branding was, as one commentator put it, 'past its sell-by date'.

The prediction of the death of brands is not entirely new. In 1991, for example, *Advertising Age* published a long and well-researched article, 'Brands in trouble – as brand loyalty crumbles, marketers look for new answers' (Liesse, 1991). As long ago as the 1970s Stephen King of J Walter Thompson (JWT) London published a pamphlet, *Crisis in Branding*, making a number of the same points. But the story that went the rounds in 1993 was triggered by one dramatic event, to which journalists added a number of other current themes to build up a picture of crisis.

The dramatic event came to be known as 'Marlboro Friday'. On 2 April 1993, Philip Morris, the world's biggest consumer products group, cut the price of its best-selling cigarette by 20%, in response to Marlboro's continued loss of share to discount brands. Philip Morris shares immediately collapsed, followed not only by other tobacco companies, but also by many other consumer goods marketers. The *Wall Street Journal* wrote:

'For makers of all consumer goods, Philip Morris's action is a milestone in marketing, the most dramatic evidence yet of a fundamental shift in consumer buying habits... More and more, shoppers are bypassing household names for the cheaper, no-name products one shelf over. This shows that even the biggest and strongest brands in the world are vulnerable.'

(Shapiro, 1993)

Suddenly a number of other themes were brought in to explain and justify what was happening. The recession had educated consumers to look for value for money. The nineties consumers were more sophisticated and discriminating, and had a different set of values from the 'materialistic' and ostentatious consumers of the eighties – they wanted *real* quality, not flashy brand names. Media fragmentation was increasingly making it impossible to advertise to them effectively *en masse*. Research showed a long-term decline in measures of brand loyalty. The retail trade was concentrating and becoming more powerful: discount warehouses in the United States, and supermarkets with highly evolved own brands in the UK. Major manufacturers were rationalising their brand portfolios, and laying off large numbers in their marketing departments. All these notions were rolled together into a general conclusion that premium brands were no longer sustainable; and when in July, Procter and Gamble (P&G) announced a 15% cut on list price across their range of detergents with a promise of 'everyday low pricing' this was seen as the final piece of evidence that brands had no future.

This conclusion was, of course, an absurd generalisation. It lumped all brands in all consumer markets together, with the added implication that branding itself was at risk (although virtually all the evidence was drawn from a few highly competitive, packaged-goods markets). It seemed to imply a global phenomenon, while confusing the very different retail circumstances of the USA, the UK and Europe. It took some observable facts and imposed questionable interpretations on them, and added some other claims which can only be regarded as speculative. All this is now, perhaps, being recognised; it was only a matter of time before journalists started to produce headlines such as, 'Brands fight back', and 'Brands are alive and kicking'. (Our title, referring to Mark Twain's remark that 'reports of my death have been greatly exaggerated', has already been used so often elsewhere that we wish we'd thought of something more original.)

It's still worth making another attempt to disentangle the real issues facing brands today from the popular myth and the rhetoric. What we hope we can show from this is a better understanding of what branding actually is and how it works – that brands are always, in a sense 'under threat', and only those that manage themselves correctly over the long term will survive. There are some particular circumstances changing at present, to which brand managers do need to find responses – but ultimately, we will argue, the concept of branding is not likely to change because it is rooted in the fundamental needs of the consumer, and because it still offers the most powerful framework for creating sustainable competitive advantage to any manufacturer or service provider.

## Reflections on Marlboro Friday

The Marlboro price cut was an extremely bold and controversial move. Commentators are still divided about its long-term consequences, and whether it should be considered as a strategic or a tactical act. The facts, however, need to be remembered. In recent years Marlboro, in common with other leading cigarette brands in the USA, had been taking annual price increases some 4% ahead of inflation. As a result, full price brands were selling at over $2 a pack while substitutable products were available for as little as 69 cents, and the brand was losing share at the rate of half a per cent a month. Meanwhile, President Clinton's aggressive anti-smoking stance looked set to impose major tax increases (up from 25 cents to $1 a pack) which threatened to push the retail price of Marlboro way beyond what most smokers would stand. All this, in a market in a long-term and inexorable decline (although tobacco consumption is still showing healthy, or perhaps one should say, unhealthy growth in many other parts of the world.) Given all this, some kind of price correction seems to have been inevitable – and necessary for the long-term survival of the brand.

What this should remind us all is that even the strongest brands cannot expect to sustain indefinite price increases. As John Philip Jones has pointed out: 'Oligopolists, like any other businesspeople, will endeavour to price their products at what the market will bear... In practice, their ability to force up prices is limited, because the elasticity of substitution between their output and that of their competitors tends to be high' (Jones, 1986, p. 27). One does not need to posit a new 'sophisticated' consumer or even a recession to explain why overpricing will create a business opportunity for anyone who can produce a parity product at a more realistic price.

On the contrary, the remarkable phenomenon that we should observe about brands in general is the extent to which they *do* continue to command a premium price. Recent analysis by Simon Broadbent of the UK grocery market – where 'own label' has taken a substantial share – shows that the leading brand in each category commands, on average, a 45% premium over the retailer own brand product (Marquis, 1994).

That does not mean that a brand has the right to charge whatever it likes. Ed Artzt of P&G has been quoted in *Fortune* (Sellers, 1993) saying that, in most markets, P&G starts to lose market share when its prices are 30–50% above store brands. But that's still a respectable premium.

Some practical definitions of brand equity (see Chapter 3) are based on the notion of premium pricing, and it is easy to see why. Premium price is one manifestation (and a practically measurable one) of the added value that a brand offers the consumer. The added value is a product of everything the brand has done over the years, including advertising. But price premium is not *synonymous* with brand strength; there are, after all, strong brands (e.g. Mars bars, Wal-Mart) which do not have to charge a premium price, because of their economies of scale. And a fascination with price premium can easily become debased into the view that you can always strengthen your brand by putting the price up; or, conversely, that a cut in price signifies a collapse in brand strength.

# Retail developments

Changes taking place in the grocery retail trade are among the most obvious and genuinely important phenomena affecting manufacturer brands. There are three main developments here, and their relative importance varies geographically.

(1) **The concentration of the retail trade** into a few major chains, which increasingly gives them the balance of power in any negotiation. This is a long-term development in all markets, but much more advanced in the UK where five retailers now account for over 60% of the business.

Power is further conferred on the retailer by the superior information now available to them through scanning technology. This is most advanced in the USA and UK.

(2) **The increased volumes sold as retailers' own brand.** This too is most advanced in the UK where own brand now accounts for 36% of packaged goods turnover. This is a long-term trend that has been developing over 20 years or more, and there has been no recent acceleration in it. It has come about partly from the growth of J Sainsbury (who always sold around 60% of own brand goods), and the progressive introduction of own brand into all the other major chains – Tesco, Safeway, Asda.

Because retailers control distribution channels and can avoid many of the marketing costs facing manufacturers (advertising can be spread across all product fields), and because they tend to invest little in R&D (with the exception of Marks and Spencer, most of their products *copy* existing brands), they can afford to offer comparable products at a considerably cheaper price. David Webster of Argyll has been quoted as saying that retailers can sell own-label products 15% cheaper than brands and still make the same cash profit. And it is possible to source high-quality products. One recent success story is the Cott Corporation who began buying cola concentrate from Royal Crown Cola and supplying a high-quality cola drink to retailers, which took share from Coke and Pepsi. Not surprisingly, the trend to own brands is growing in the USA and in Europe, and stores such as Wal-Mart, which started by discounting brands, are now discovering the opportunities offered by own label.

The more successful retailer brands, far from competing on price alone, themselves offer a strong degree of brand reassurance. Carrefour, in France, is highly committed to its own brands and aims for higher quality than the branded products. Retailers may now offer own-brand products at two or three different price/quality levels – the French chain, Auchan, offers four levels.

Another aspect of the 'death of brands' debate was a controversy in the UK over the extent to which supermarkets closely copied the pack format and visual codes of successful brands. This came to a head with Sainsbury's launch of 'Classic Cola', a look-alike (Cott-sourced) Coke which, after some legal sparring, they agreed to modify. (Such imitation itself says a great deal about the power of the visual imagery of brands, although it is a form of flattery that manufacturers no doubt feel they could do without.)

(3) **The growth of discount retailers and discount brands**, such as Wal-Mart in the USA, or Aldi and Netto in Europe. This differs from the retailer own brand in so far as the main promise is price alone, offering a limited range of sometimes obscure brands with invented names with no heritage, but at prices which open the gap between them and the established brand names still wider. Heinz Baked Beans at 29p per tin may have had a hard time competing with own labels at 25p, but this was nothing compared with discount brands selling as a loss leader at 16p. It was against such 'generic' priced cigarettes that Marlboro found itself in an increasingly untenable position.

## Advertising and sales promotion

We hear a lot today about 'media fragmentation'. It is true, especially in the USA, that the increased number of TV Channels, radio stations, and print titles has made it more difficult to reach a mass market audience – but it has not made it impossible. What has really made mass market advertising a weaker force in recent years in the USA, has been the reluctance of clients to spend money on it. The proportion of marketing spend put into sales promotion instead of advertising has grown from less than half to around three-quarters – and sales promotion nowadays means deep discount price-cutting, and other incentives to the retailer to give display space.

The trend towards discounting in the USA, where brand shares yo-yo up and down from week to week depending on promotions, has certainly not helped the long-term health of brands caught in the cycle. It has also been instrumental in eroding patterns of brand loyalty. DDB's Lifestyle Study shows how fewer people now claim to buy the same brand every time. Considering what is happening to the price and display of brands in store, this is hardly surprising. However, the phenomenon is not consumer-led, but manufacturer-led.

One particular irony is that P&G's 'everyday low price' policy, cited as evidence of brands' weakness, was an attempt to break out of this destructive cycle of an unrealistic list price heavily discounted from time to time, to establish a stable price which would not be subject to deep price-cutting. As such it was a move to protect and strengthen brands – the opposite of how it was popularly portrayed. (Other companies such as General Mills have since followed a similar path.)

To return to media fragmentation: yes, this is a real phenomenon. Most advanced in the USA, but developing now in Europe, it will make it more difficult to reach a mass market cheaply. It is too early to say whether this will result in advertisers deserting traditional mass media in favour of direct mail – despite its much greater cost per impact – or the emergent 'interactive' media. What we do see at the moment, however, is a renewed interest in TV on the part of brand owners. Evidence from AGB (Buck, 1993) shows a correlation between weight of commercial TV viewing and propensity to buy manufacturer brands. Moreover, media expenditure, at least in markets which are emerging from recession, is once more growing in real terms.

TV may become a more expensive option, but it would be surprising if major advertisers were to desert it; it is simply too powerful as a brand-building medium. Besides, a certain critical mass will be needed to afford TV, and that will favour big brands – and of course, retailers.

## The rationalisation of brands – and of brand managers

Another story which was brought in to add to the 'death of brands' hypothesis is that some major manufacturers have been reducing the number of brands they market. P&G and Unilever have both recently announced programmes to reduce the number of lines they sell by 20%. For instance, last year P&G withdrew 7 of 17 lines in the Luvs range, one third of Camay sub-products, and divested Clarion cosmetics and Citrus Hill fruit juice. The Danone Group in France rationalised the L'Alsacienne brand under the Belin name in the cookie market, and dropped the Gervais yoghurt brand to concentrate on Danone.

However, these decisions again need to be seen in context. The total number of lines available in most consumer markets has exploded. The number of lines stocked in a typical American supermarket has doubled in the last ten years. Twenty years ago, the UK Nielsen Toilet Tissue audit listed 11 lines – today it has 460. (This in itself may be an important factor to remember when considering claims of declining brand loyalty.)

Brand manufacturers are in a paradoxical situation, but not a new one. They know that continued brand success requires innovation, so they continually strive to identify new marketing segments and target them. Yet the economics of branding have generally depended on scale economies; the hidden costs of an endlessly proliferating range of products and/or brands in inventory, production economies, management time, and promotional expenditure can end up being ruinous. Once again, it is for the long-term health of manufacturer brands that they need from time to time to weed out products and brands which no longer have a real reason for their existence. Add to this the increasing trend towards international marketing strategies and the pressure put by own labels on traditional third or second brands without a strong point of difference, and it seems obvious that major manufacturers such as P&G or Unilever need to make clearances.

The decline in numbers of people employed in marketing departments was also misrepresented as part of the 'death of brands' saga. It seems true that many marketing departments have been restructured in recent years, with reductions in size. However, what this reflects (apart from general corporate downsizing in all departments) is a widespread dissatisfaction with marketing departments' effectiveness, not with the idea of brand marketing itself. Coopers & Lybrand (1994) concluded that, 'Marketing departments undertake an ill defined mixture of activities which could often be delegated to other functions, or dispensed with altogether.' Paradoxically, as 'marketing' itself becomes more important, companies are recognising that it involves key decisions right across the organisation. The death of the brand manager is far from signalling the death of brands.

## The price-conscious consumer

Generalisations about changes in consumer attitudes are often largely speculative, whatever bits of research evidence may be produced to back them up. A number of theories were put forward to suggest that people in the 1990s would be less ostentatious, more concerned with true spiritual values, more concerned with value for money, more discriminating, more sensitive to price. At the extreme the French group Comfreca created *Le Deconsommation*, in which consumers would turn away completely from the materialistic excesses of the 1980s and refuse to consume.

Such generalisations are always dubious: partly because people are increasingly heterogeneous, and partly because it is difficult to find real evidence to support such sweeping statements. (Such media myths can also become self-fulfilling; perhaps the only thing one could say with confidence about the nineties is that it was the first decade in which everyone claimed to know what its prevailing values were to be before it had even started. Consumer quotes often have the air of recycled newspaper articles). If such claims of non-materialism do reflect real phenomena, they are more likely to be environmentally driven than coming from a shift in the *zeitgeist*; for instance, attitudes to pricing will be modified by the existence of discounted alternatives, and perceived patterns of brand-buying behaviour will be affected by deep discounting and proliferation of choice.

What we can do, with specific reference to this hypothesis of the death of brands, is to ask two questions:

(1) Do we need to hypothesise a shift in consumer value systems in order to explain what we observe to be happening?
(2) What consumer needs did brands satisfy in the first place, and are these of a sort that is likely to change?

## Have consumer value systems changed?

'People increasingly buy goods on price, not because they carry a famous name.'

(*The Economist*, 9 April 1994)

In fact much of the 'evidence' which was adduced to demonstrate the change in consumer attitudes has already been discussed – Marlboro Friday, the rise of retailer brands and discounting, the claimed decline in loyal buyer behaviour – and in each case the true story relates to changes on the supply side, such as price rises, competitive initiatives, proliferation of lines; but is there other evidence for changes in consumer attitudes?

The Henley Centre (1994) argues that 'demand for lower prices has intensified over the course of the recession', quoting survey results that show more consumers are looking for lower prices and some rather more tendentious econometric analysis that suggests that price elasticities in certain product fields have increased. Indeed, given the economic uncertainties affecting a wide spectrum of the population, it would be surprising if this weren't substantially true. Nevertheless, the same report shows that demands for better service and better quality have *also* increased in most product fields – implying that if there is a trend, it is not towards buying on price alone, but a more conscious determination to get value for money. Another question shows that the numbers of people who agree that 'highest price equals highest quality' have declined since peaking in 1989. But one of the biggest shifts is in the number agreeing, 'It's best to buy the nationally advertised and well known brands because you can rely on their quality', which went up from 37% in 1981 to 54% in 1993.

A similar question, asked on the DDB Lifestyle Survey in the USA – 'I try to stick to well known brand names' – dipped during the recession in 1992 but picked up again in 1993: 60% of respondents then agreed, a similar level to the first half of the eighties. Other questions on the same survey show long-term trends that are the opposite of what the writers on the *Wall Street Journal* might have led us to expect. Numbers agreeing that 'A store's own brand is usually a better buy than a nationally advertised brand' have steadily trended *downwards* since 1981, and among women the proportion is today close to the all time low. Furthermore, agreement with the statement 'I always check prices even on small items' is either static or in a long-term decline, depending which time-scale you look at.

Another analysis from France (Degon, 1994) argues that consumers are not simply looking for the cheapest product in a market, but are identifying many different levels of quality and price, and choosing between them; it is only within very narrow bands of comparable products that price becomes a discriminator.

It is hard, therefore, to find hard evidence for *The Economist*'s 'more price conscious consumer'. There may be slightly more truth in the story of the 'more demanding consumer', driven by the real effects of recession and a certain cynicism about the excesses, real or perceived, of some aspects of the 1980s. Still, that is at best a tendency, and not, as sometimes portrayed, a fundamental revolution in attitudes. Value for money, the pleasure of getting a bargain, healthy cynicism about manufacturers, a disinclination to pay excessive premiums for parity or inferior products – surely, none of these is an exclusively new concern. It seems we are far too ready to imagine previous decades as ones in which naïve consumers allowed themselves to be ripped off by unscrupulous manufacturers offering nothing but clever ads and fancy packages.

The real problem in the 1980s was that too many *brand owners* came to believe that clever ads and fancy packages were all they needed. Many manufacturers, far from working to innovate and improve quality, were mainly concerned with reducing cost – and, as we saw with Marlboro, often inflating the price at the same time. Tod Johnson of the US product testing consultancy, the NPD Group, was quoted in *Advertising Age*:

> 'When we tested products in the 60s and 70s, I'd say 75% of the changes were product improvements. Today, two thirds or even three quarters of the testing we do is asking for consumer opinions on cost reductions. Product quality is being ignored.'
>
> (Liesse, 1991)

Brands are not a con trick that has only just been found out. If they were, they would deserve to die the death so often predicted for them; but consumers were never so naïve. They bought brands because those brands offered them satisfactions they couldn't get elsewhere. We now need to go back and examine what those consumer benefits of branding are, and what the nature of the brand 'contract' between consumer and manufacturer ought to be.

## The consumer benefits of branding

A strong brand offers numerous benefits to its owner: stability, profitability, resistance to competitive attack, and a platform for innovation. Yet branding would not have become such a powerful marketing concept unless it also offered real benefits to the consumer. The benefits can be considered under the following headings:

- A badge of origin/proof of authenticity
- A promise of performance
- A transformation of the user experience
- A symbolic language – internal and external

### *A badge of origin/proof of authenticity*

A brand – originally, a mark burnt on to a beast or a barrel – served to prove ownership or provenance, and in marketing terms, the history of branding is closely tied up with the history of trade mark law, a fact which we very much take for granted, but which is still of considerable importance. We accept it as proof that a jar sold as Hellmann's mayonnaise is, indeed, Hellmann's mayonnaise, and not an inferior imitation: an important benefit to the buyer who would otherwise have to approach purchasing decisions in quite a different way. A hundred years ago manufacturers still felt it necessary to make pack designs as complex as banknotes to avoid forgery and, like banknotes, some even carried a facsimile of the founder's signature. When trade mark law is infringed, as in the counterfeit designer perfumes or Lacoste shirts which are imported from the Far East, it not only unsettles the consumer, but it changes the meanings that these symbols ought to possess. All the added values of branding, then, depend upon this belief in authenticity being maintained. Fake items may deceive other people, but they won't fool the purchaser.

### *A promise of performance*

Given the authenticity of the brand, the buyer has learned to expect that the product inside will be consistent – that Hellmann's mayonnaise will taste the same from one jar to the next, and that if it fails to do so, it will be cause for complaint and redress. This is not a logically necessary condition of branding, but it has become fairly universal in its acceptance, so even when brands, as they frequently do, make improvements to their products, they announce the fact clearly. Consistency is important to consumers; it means they can confidently replicate a satisfactory experience, and it is therefore an important part of the brand promise. To default on the promise can be seen as a breach of contract which will not easily be forgiven, the classic example being the relaunch of Coca-Cola with its new formula.

This has two implications for marketers. First, the management of change, which is frequently necessary, needs to be handled with care and within a framework of keeping the larger promise of the brand. (In some product fields, of course, the product itself changes every day, such as newspapers, but they are nevertheless strongly branded.) Second, the brand's strength is not separable from the product or service delivery. A luxury car with the best 'image' around can rapidly become undesirable, if the quality of the engineering lets it down (as happened with Jaguar in the 1970s). Furthermore, the cost reductions beloved of marketing departments in recent years will eventually jeopardise a brand, even if they proceed by imperceptible steps. In the 1960s Cadbury's Dairy Milk progressively reduced the thickness of its chocolate bar, and the devaluing of the product was only revealed when competitor Rowntree's launched a new, thick bar, 'Yorkie'.

## A transformation of the user experience

The promise of performance is more than just an aid to decision-making. It actually enhances the value of the product. Consumers will pay extra for the knowledge that the product will not let them down: that a washing machine will not break down, that a detergent will get the clothes clean, that the family will eat the ready meal. Anticipation, and peace of mind, are both potentially important parts of the user experience.

We have all seen examples of the blind vs. branded product test. Typically, this shows that two products which receive parity scores when tasted unbranded, exhibit a clear preference pattern when in their branded packs. This demonstrates something we can recognise from our own experience – our experience is heavily conditioned by beliefs or suggestions. Extensive medical literature attests to the extent of the placebo effect, where a chemically inert substance presented as a drug can have powerful effects on physical symptoms. One experiment has shown how branding (in analgesics) creates its own version of placebo effect – patients claimed their own preferred brand was 25% more effective at relieving pain than a chemically identical unbranded product (Branthwaite & Cooper, 1981).

The satisfactions which people pay for when they choose Marlboro, Heinz or Coca-Cola may not be entirely created by physical product differences, but they are nevertheless real.

### A symbolic language – internal and external

We tend to take for granted (unless we are semioticians) the power of names and symbols in structuring our lives. Choices we make, in food and drink, clothes, decorating our homes, cars, cigarettes, all have a meaning for us and often for others, which goes far beyond the merely functional. This is universally true in all societies in all ages, and would be true if brands did not exist. Brands are simply another set of codes, on to which, inevitably, consumers project their own meanings.

It is part of the opportunity for the brand owner to control the meaning that the brand has for people. Lucozade, sold for years as an energy drink for convalescents, came to evoke feeble people, invalids and children – a meaning which was changed when the brand was repositioned as an energy drink for sports.

It is this symbolic level of brand meaning which some commentators in the 1990s claimed was about to disappear, quoting as examples fashionable and expensive brands from the 1980s which the 'new, realistic' nineties consumer no longer wanted. A Hiram Walker executive said: 'A few years ago it might have been considered smart to wear a shirt with a designer's logo embroidered on the pocket: frankly, it now seems a bit naff' (*The Guardian*, 12 June 1993). Although fashions may come and go, 'fashion' itself seems to be part of our social condition. There may be a time when it is important to some people *not* to choose Louis Vuitton luggage; but this does not mean the name has lost meaning.

## Brands – are they still important?

It is time to pull together the strands of the argument so far, before outlining implications for the marketers of brands.

We hope we have shown that, on the whole, the story about the 'death of brands' was journalistic exaggeration and misrepresentation. In fact, the most dramatic evidence of the death of brands – Marlboro Friday – was largely irrelevant to the real issue, which is that of retailer power.

Because of the growing power of retailers, manufacturer brands in packaged goods face an increasingly difficult environment. It is too early to see where this trend ultimately leads, but it seems unlikely that either consumers or indeed retailers themselves would be happy with a future in which manufacturer brands had no role.

Consumers are demanding, and discriminating, and can't be fooled for long, but whether this is anything new is more debatable. One possible new element is a growing consumer interest in environmental and ethical issues, although experience to date suggests this will remain secondary to more functional considerations. It may however be an emerging factor which will lead to more emphasis on corporate, rather than product, brands.

However, none of this points to 'the end of the road for brands' – not in packaged goods, and still less in all the other areas where brands matter, such as durables, cars, financial services, retailing. In some categories, takeaway food for instance, branding is obviously on the increase; but what we can take from this debate is a renewed understanding of what brands are really about. Brands whose owners understand and act on this are likely to survive; others, ultimately, may not.

## Implications for managing brands

The four implications listed are important for the brand owner:

(1)  The promise that the brand represents must be based in reality – quality, innovation, service, ethics.
(2)  Differentiation from other brands must be at a deeper level than mere packaging and advertising (although these reflect it).
(3)  Achieving the right balance between consistency and change.
(4)  Realisation that the active brand, not the passive brand, will succeed.

### The promise of the brand

A dangerous belief seemed to arise during the 1980s that a brand name is some sort of magic talisman which is somehow sufficient, on its own, to suspend the normal laws of consumer marketing. It is easy to see how this happened. There are many examples nowadays of famous brands which are still able to command a premium price for essentially parity products. This phenomenon leads both the enthusiasts and the ethical critics of brand marketing to claim that people are 'merely paying for the name'. It is a step from this to believing that the name alone has an enormous value, which can be separated from the company and product it represents. This was hyped enormously in the late 1980s when Nestlé bought Rowntree for a sum several times the value of its tangible assets, leading just about every commentator to claim that the difference must be the value of the brand names. It would be more accurate to suppose that Nestlé bought Rowntree because they believed they could manage the business more profitably, exploit synergies between the two companies, and in particular develop a market for Rowntree products across Europe – where they were at the time largely unknown (so much for brand equity).

Excessive belief in the magic of brand names is highly dangerous in the long term for the brand owner. The most useful way to see the 'death of brands' story is as a healthily sceptical reaction against this belief. In the short term it is usually possible to exploit the trust and the image that a brand has built up over the years. In the early 1970s Cadbury's Smash (the first brand in the UK instant mashed potato market) was threatened by Wondermash, launched with an obviously superior product format which it would take some time for Smash to even copy. Because of the loyalty which the Cadbury's brand had already built up, trial of the new brand, even with couponing, was disappointingly low and Cadbury's had time to reformulate before their share was eroded. However, the value of such brand strength is simply to buy time. The famous brands that we see around us in packaged goods, almost without exception, built their reputations on innovation, often by creating a whole new category – Kellogg inventing the concept of breakfast cereal, King Gillette the safety razor, John Pemberton popularising a carbonated herbal tonic called Coca-Cola. They then prospered by continuing to innovate or improve quality or maintain a level of value that competitors could not match. Once the investment in innovation and quality stops, the brand is in danger. Unilever, Procter & Gamble, and Gillette know this well – but if you look at brands that are really in trouble today, you will generally find products that have lost competitive advantage through devaluation or just failure to innovate, and yet still expect to command an ever-widening price gap against parity competitors.

### Differentiation from other brands

Differentiation from other brands needs to be at a deeper level than mere packaging and advertising, which implies that, although there is a definite and valuable element of 'goodwill' attached to a brand name, it is not usually separable from the reality it stands for. Therefore we should expect that managing a brand is about more than the external communications of packaging and advertising. Yet the brand is not the same as any one physical product. Products almost inevitably change over time, sometimes quite radically; Fairy originally was a solid bar of soap, now it is a washing-up liquid, and of course, many brand names are used across a range of different products. Heinz long ago exceeded its 57 varieties; at the most extreme, in

Japan, corporate brands such as Yamaha span such different products as motorcycles and musical instruments.

Neither is the brand usually synonymous with the legal or corporate entity that owns it. Kraft is different from Kraft General Foods – Schweppes is not the same as Cadbury Schweppes. So what is a brand?

We think that it is most helpful to conceptualise a brand as a particular sense of 'meaning and direction', with which the customer can develop a relationship through the products, services, and communications which this directs. If we consider some successful brands created in the 1990s – Apple, Body Shop, Häagen Dazs, Phileas Fogg (in itself a list which should give the lie to any suggestion that brands were becoming obsolete) – it is clear that in each case a coherent purpose and value system can be inferred from everything these brands do. It can also be inferred that this 'brand identity' precedes the development of product as well as communications, while giving a maximum degree of freedom to each brand to adapt, react, and grow.

## Balance between consistency and change

This way of conceptualising the brand offers a solution to a long-standing difficulty of brand management. On the one hand, there is the tendency of established brands to ossify because of a reluctance to change design, product or methods, often reinforced by market research which defines the brand in terms of its existing 'image' in the minds of consumers, and thus creates a closed circle from which the brand cannot escape. Such 'ossification' makes it impossible for the brand to respond to changing circumstances. On the other hand there is the opposite danger – that the pressure to change will lead management to abandon the implicit values which made the brand successful, and therefore destroy the relationship with the consumer that has been built up. By understanding the brand identity as a start point for all action, tactical freedom can be reconciled with consistency.

## The active brand and success

In today's increasingly competitive environment, it is important for brand management to begin with a clear, shared understanding throughout the organisation and its agencies of what a brand's identity, central meaning and purpose are. These are not to be arrived at passively with reference to existing consumer beliefs or current products, rather a proactive stance is necessary, looking both backwards to the brand's history and origins, and forwards to the future environment in which the brand needs to define its role.

To assist in this process DDB uses a conceptual framework and methodology called Brand Foundations™. This is not a packaging or advertising brief; it comes before specific communication tasks and is about the overall identity of the brand. It ensures that specific briefs, when they are needed, can be fulfilled with reference to the brand's overall development as well as the specific communication task.

The process is conceptually simple: it involves finding agreed, coherent, and stimulating answers to a number of questions:

- The origin, founding myth or 'anchorage'
- The brand's area of competence and skill
- The brand's point of difference from others
- The imagined customer of the brand, and what it means to them to be the brand's client
- What the brand fights for
- The brand's personality
- The key value underlying the brand

The process is consensual. It draws on consumer research, market research and predictions for future developments of the market environment as well as on the past history of the brand, its products and presentation; but it also develops from the company's internal culture and the views and ambitions of the individuals involved, and the company's skills and resources. Consultants review internal and external research sources, including those relating to the brand's history, and also interview as many people as possible within the organisation to understand both its culture and its strengths. Findings and interpretation are fed back to a steering committee including senior managers in a series of debriefs, leading to a brainstorming session in which answers to the key questions can be created and agreed. The last necessary stage is the implementation of the brand foundations throughout the organisation and its agencies.

## Conclusion

The story of 'the death of brands' was misleading and exaggerated, but it may serve to remind us that branding is not a magical device for charging inflated prices for undifferentiated products; it is a relationship of trust and not, in the long term, one which can be abused. Through a brand's actions and communications, consumers will know what it stands for, and ultimately judge it. It is important, therefore, for those managing brands, to begin by defining their own sense of mission and values for the brand.

# References

Branthwaite, A. & Cooper, P. (1981) Analgesic effects of branding in treatment of headaches. *British Medical Journal*, 282.

Buck, S. (1993) Will advertising save brands from the own-label threat? *Marketing*, 2nd April, p. 17.

Coopers & Lybrand (1994) *Marketing at the Crossroads*. Coopers & Lybrand, London.

Degon, R. (1994) La Société du Sens: Un nouveau regard sur les Prix. In *Les marques et le consommateur*. IREP (Institut de Récherches et d'Études Publicitaires), Paris.

Henley Centre (1994) *Planning for Social Change 1993/94*, Volume 2. Henley Centre, London.

Jones, J.P. (1986) *What's in a Name? Advertising and the Concept of Brands*. Lexington Books, Lexington, Massachusetts.

Liesse, J. (1991) Brands in trouble – as brand loyalty crumbles, marketers look for new answers. *Advertising Age*, 2nd December.

Marquis, S. (1994) Alive and kicking. *Marketing*, 7th April, pp. 8–9.

Sellers, P. (1993) Brands: it's thrive or die. *Fortune*, 23rd August, pp. 40–44.

Shapiro, G. (1993) Cigarette burn: price cut on Marlboro upsets rosy notions about tobacco profits. *Wall Street Journal*, 5th April p. A1.

## Afterword

Six years later, I have seen no evidence to contradict the original conclusions of this chapter. The DDB Lifestyle Survey in the USA has continued to track the attitude statements quoted and it is worth looking at what has happened since 1995:

'I try to stick to well known brand names' has remained, overall, around 66% for men and 56% for women, with no clear trend up or down.

'A store's own brand is usually a better buy than a nationally advertised brand' hovers around 58% for both women and men. The figure for men did rise to a high of 64% in 2000, possibly indicating an upward trend, though it dropped again in 2001.

'I always check prices, even on small items' remains almost flat for women at about 81%, but does appear to trend upward for men from a low point in 1998 of 52% to 57% in 2001.

These findings continue a general pattern of stability dating back to the 1970s, with one exception: the number of consumers claiming to stick to well-known brand names did drop sharply during the recession of the early 1980s, from an overall 75% to 61%, which is pretty much where it has stayed ever since.

With the popularity of books like Naomi Klein's *No Logo* and the public criticism of brands such as Nike and Starbucks, it is likely that another 'death of brands' story is brewing. As in 1993, it will be important to look at what's not changing, as well as what is, before jumping to overdramatic conclusions. Even the best-loved and admired brands can fail, for all kinds of reasons. But I stick by my assertions that whether you like it or not, the basic principles of branding will always be with us.

## Chapter 3

# What is Brand Equity, Anyway, and How do You Measure it?

'What is the answer to the question being asked in cocktail lounges, all the time, all over America – "What is Brand Equity anyway, and how do you measure it?"'

Thornton C. Lockwood, Communications Research Manager, AT&T, 1994

## Introduction – from brand image to brand equity

Brands have been a major aspect of marketing reality for more than a hundred years. The *theory* of branding is much more recent. David Ogilvy was talking about the importance of brand image as early as 1951 (quoted in Biel, 1993), but it was first fully articulated by Burleigh Gardner and Sidney Levy in their classic *Harvard Business Review* paper (1955). Despite such authoritative origins, the concept of brand image remained, until recently, peripheral to the mainstream of advertising theory and evaluation. While it was endorsed from the 1960s onward by the British Account Planning movement (King, 1970; Cowley, 1989), it was regarded by many advertisers and researchers (especially in the United States) as a rather woolly theory – the sort of thing advertising agency people talked airily about when they failed to 'get a hard product message across' or to 'convert prospects' or to 'make sales', as they were supposed to be doing. Brand image became associated with expressions like the 'soft sell' (Reeves, 1961) and the 'weak theory of advertising' (Jones, 1991), giving it the air of a whimsical luxury that a business-like advertiser could hardly afford.

Originally published as 'Do we really need "brand equity"?', *Journal of Brand Management*, 1996, 4(1), pp. 9–28. Permission for using this material has been granted by Henry Stewart Publications, Museum House, 25 Museum Street, London WC1A 1JT, www.henrystewart.co.uk.

Then in the 1980s the hard-nosed business people began to notice that brands appeared to be changing hands for huge sums of money! As takeover fever spread, the difference between balance sheet valuations and the prices paid by predators was substantially attributed to 'the value of brands'. Suddenly, the brand stopped being an obscure metaphysical concept of dubious relevance. It was something that was worth money.

This shift of perception was reflected in the way that the traditional expression 'brand *image*' (with its suggestion of a ghostly illusion), was increasingly displaced by its more solid financial equivalent, 'brand equity'. It is not clear who invented the expression, but few uses of it have been traced before the middle of the 1980s (Ambler & Styles, 1995). It achieved respectability when it was taken up by the prestigious Marketing Science Institute, who held a major seminar on the subject in 1988, and has been going strong ever since.

In fact, the past few years have seen brand equity become one of the hottest topics in business. In America, there is a now an influential body, the Coalition for Brand Equity, founded in 1991, which evangelises for the importance of building brand relationships and brand loyalty. Interesting (and very different) books have been published on the subject (Aaker, 1991; Kapferer, 1992). It has spawned numerous conferences and seminars. It has attracted a lot of interest from academic researchers, although the greatest part of their work has been connected with brand equity as applied to brand extensions (Barwise, 1993). Meanwhile commercial researchers have been busily designing and selling methods for measuring, tracking, and optimising brand equity.

This can be seen as something of a paradigm shift in marketing thinking, and in my view a positive one. It seems right that the ideas formulated by Gardner and Levy, and by King, so long ago, should at last be granted legitimacy as a serious part of business. In the conclusions to this chapter I shall review the positive aspects of brand equity, but while I joined the cheering crowds lining the great brand equity parade, I was still bothered by two questions that did not seem to have clear enough answers.

(1)  What exactly is meant by the term brand equity – and does it mean the same thing to everybody?
(2)  How far can brand equity be measured in an objective way?

The answers I have found raise some further questions:

(1)  Is brand equity a useful concept?
(2)  Is brand equity, in fact, needed at all?

## The three senses of brand equity

Karl Popper warned against a common mistake made by philosophers, which he called 'essentialism'. The mistake is supposing that you will find the truth by starting with a word and arguing about what it 'really' means, but words, as Humpty Dumpty suggested, mean just what their users want them to mean. They can have various meanings, and it is pointless to argue about which is 'right' or 'wrong'. When a common expression *does* have distinct meanings, however, it as well to be aware of the fact so as to avoid unnecessary confusion. This is true of the term brand equity, which seems to be used in three quite distinct senses (each of which has several further nuances of meaning):

(1) The total value of a brand as a separable asset – when it is sold, or included on a balance sheet
(2) A measure of the strength of consumers' attachment to a brand
(3) A description of the associations and beliefs the consumer has about the brand

Of these three concepts, the first could less ambiguously be called brand valuation (and often is). For the present argument I shall refer to it as *brand value*.

The concept of measuring the consumer's level of attachment to a brand can be called brand loyalty – although this phrase is almost as ambiguous as brand equity itself. I prefer *brand strength* for this sense, and, although I am aware that this is also potentially confusing, that is what I shall call it in this chapter.

The third concept could be called by the traditional name of brand image but, for clarity, here I shall call it *brand description*. This reflects its fundamental difference from the other two senses of brand equity; it is unlike them because we would not expect it to be represented by a single number.

Brand value could also be seen as the odd one out in another way, as it refers to an actual or notional *business* transaction, whereas the other two focus on the consumer. In fact, brand strength and brand description are sometimes referred to as *consumer brand equity* to distinguish them from the asset valuation meaning.

Although it should already be clear that these three concepts are different, it is tempting to assume that they are closely related to each other. Brand strength could be a key determinant of the overall brand value; brand description might be expected to affect, or at least to explain, the brand strength. Underlying much of the talk about brand equity, and some of the more elaborate proposals for measuring it, such as the Yankelovich methodology (Taylor, 1992), seems to be the assumption of a causal chain along the following lines:

One theme to be pursued in this chapter is to show why both the links in this chain are weak, or at best, obscure. This being the case, there are clear dangers in using the same name for all three (or even any two) of these concepts – it gives the impression (deliberately or through carelessness) that they are all aspects of the same thing. Like the arrows in the above diagram, calling them all brand equity is an easy way to create the illusion that an operational relationship exists which, in reality, cannot be demonstrated.

These three meanings of brand equity are distinct concepts which require separate discussion. If we are talking about three different things, there are three different questions about measurement. Brand description, in a sense, is not something we should expect to measure at all in the sense of a single scale, though of course brand attributes can be 'measured' using multiple scales. I therefore deal with this here fairly briefly, but cover it further in Chapter 4. The lengthiest discussion is of brand strength, as this seems to me what most of the brand equity debates have centred on. However, it is also necessary to review the area of brand value, although I do not go into any of the financial ramifications of this much discussed topic. These have been reviewed at greater length by others better qualified to do so (Barwise *et al.*, 1989; Kapferer, 1992).

## Sense 1. Brand equity = brand value

The need to put a value on a brand arises for two main reasons:

(1) To set a price when the brand is sold.
(2) To include it as an intangible asset on a balance sheet, a practice which is now possible in the UK but not everywhere.[1]

It has been suggested, following from this, that the balance sheet valuation of a brand should become one of the measures by which the management of the brand (and various inputs such as advertising) can be evaluated.

---

1    The rules in the UK have changed since this was written. See the Afterword to this chapter.

Consultants have devised formulas which are now widely used for creating brand valuations, foremost among these being Interbrand and management consultancies such as Arthur Andersen (Murphy, 1990; Barrett & Bertolotti, 1992). However, there remain a number of difficulties which we should be aware of, particularly if using these formulas as an indication of a brand's overall strength or health, or as a basis for evaluating performance.

First of all there is the significant difference between an 'objective' valuation created for balance sheet purposes, and the actual price that a brand might fetch in a real sale. If we think of brands as houses, it seems reasonable to us that an expert should be able to say within quite narrow limits what a particular one might fetch – its market value. However, estate agents and surveyors are able to do this for property (not always, but most of the time) because they have many points of comparison. They have seen similar houses sold and with a little experience can form a sound idea of a 'market price', but brands are both more different and less frequently sold than houses, so the norms needed to estimate a market price do not usually exist.

More importantly, a brand is likely to have a much higher value to one purchaser than another. If a company already owns factories, manufacturing skills, means of distribution, or indeed other brands (Barwise & Robertson, 1992), there may be synergies that make it worth paying a great deal for a particular brand. To a company without the same assets, the same name could be worth relatively little. For acquisition purposes, the value of a brand to a particular purchaser is best estimated by scenario planning – what future cash flows could this company achieve if it owned and exploited that brand? Takeover prices can be higher than current valuations because these incremental cash flows might be far greater than the brand could ever deliver to the existing user.

We can think of brands in this sense as being like properties on the Monopoly board. The face value of Coventry Street is £280: but if you own the other two streets in the yellow set, and have plenty of cash to develop the set when complete, its value to you will be far more. Another player, even paying face value, would never be able to recoup their investment.

This is one reason why there is no such thing as an absolute value for a brand. What it might actually realise, if sold, depends a great deal on who might be interested in buying it at the time, and why. If two companies both want it, this might inflate the price considerably more as, in addition to the cash one could generate from the brand, is also added the strategic advantage of keeping it out of the hands of a competitor. The battle between Nestlé and Jacob Suchard to own Rowntree (perhaps the most often quoted example of 'the value of brands') is a good example of this.

Another unresolved difficulty surrounding brand valuation is the issue of *separability*. John Stuart, when Chairman of Quaker Oats Ltd, was famously quoted: 'If this business were to be split up, I would be glad to take the brands, trademarks, and goodwill, and you could have all the bricks and mortar – and I would fare better than you.' He may, in his particular case, have been right, but the claim would not always apply. A successful business does have other assets besides trade marks and bricks and mortar. Many brand names, removed from the management, the skills, the culture, the support that they normally enjoy, would rapidly lose their customer base. Again, this makes the point that a brand – essentially, the right to a particular name or identity – has a value that fluctuates according to who uses it.

Balance sheet valuations can concern themselves only with the current user, and on this basis they try to estimate the future profit stream derived from the brand and, within this, how much can be attributed to the brand name itself. The main motives for having balance sheet valuations at all are financial, and these need not be discussed here. However, it has also been argued that the act of valuing brands formally is a good discipline for a company, which will shift its attention away from a concentration on the immediate profit-and-loss account to a consideration of the longer term.

This sounds as if it should be the case, but to what extent it really works depends on the formula used to create the brand's value. The preferred methods commonly in use start by considering the brand's current profitability. They then apply probabilities to the current situation growing or continuing, based on various measures of 'brand strength', which in this sense may include consumer research and also other factors such as competitive position (Murphy, 1990). The in-depth analysis of all aspects of the brand involved may well be a valuable exercise. What is questionable is whether such approaches are looking at brand value in a pure sense, or at the business unit as a whole. As sales and, particularly, profitability can be manipulated faster and more easily than the underlying measures of brand strength (which are in any case necessarily subjective), the simplest way to increase a brand's valuation on this basis could be by continuing a short-term focus on profits; which is exactly what many advocates of brand equity are keen to get away from.

This raises another crucial issue to which I will return later – that of separating brand *strength* from brand *size*. Coca-Cola will appear a *stronger* brand than Pepsi, on most usual measures, because it is a *bigger* brand than Pepsi. One of the key issues in the whole field of brand equity measurement is finding an indication of brand strength which is not simply a tautology for brand size. One extreme view is that the two are, in fact, the same (Ehrenberg, 1993). While I disagree with this, it is certainly true that large brands, particularly market leaders, derive a great deal of competitive strength from their relative size, and that many measures of brand strength are strongly affected by brand size.

There is however an even more fundamental issue about brand valuation. The commonest (and most logical) way to estimate a brand's value is by discounting its future cash flows. This means forecasting the future. Now, forecasting is a necessary task – but it is different from objectively measuring something. To forecast, you have to make all sorts of assumptions about the future, many of which will, in the event, turn out to be wrong. That is why forecasts tend to be volatile, and why buying and selling things on the basis of forecasts (e.g. shares) has an element of gambling about it.

The American magazine *Financial World* does a valuation each year of the world's top brands. In 1992 they valued Marlboro at a very precise $51.6 billion. A year later, using the same procedures, they valued it at only $33 billion. All that had happened in between was that Marlboro had cut its price. Many observers would probably agree now that had the brand not cut its price, it faced a disastrous long-term future; in fact, the brand was 'stronger' when valued at $33 billion than when it was $51.6 billion! Certainly I do not believe it had become any less attractive to its consumers as a result of the price cut. All this should suggest to us that whatever brand valuations show, they are not objective measures of reality, nor reflections of consumer brand strength.

In summary then, a valuation for balance sheet purposes is not the same as a valuation made on behalf of a particular purchaser. Valuations are volatile, varying according to assumptions and context. They do not reflect current measures of the brand's strength with the consumer.

## Sense 2. Brand equity = brand strength: a measure of relative consumer demand for the brand

David Aaker (1991) describes brand equity as having five components:

(1)  Brand loyalty
(2)  Awareness
(3)  Perceived quality
(4)  Other associations
(5)  Other brand assets

This is a pragmatic recognition of the principal concepts that have been associated with brand strength, and that can be measured. It can be criticised for lacking an underlying theory that relates these five ideas to each other (McWilliam, 1993), but by the same token we may have to be prepared for the fact that no such underlying theory really exists.

The many different methods that have been published can, for the most part, be described as using one, or a combination, of the following basic types of measure:

(1)  Price/demand measures (including modelling approaches)
(2)  Behavioural measures of loyalty (buying behaviour)
(3)  Attitudinal measures of loyalty
(4)  Awareness/salience measures

Of these, the second is similar to Aaker's *loyalty* component, the last to his *awareness* component, while the third is related to, but not the same as, his concept of perceived quality.

Aaker's brand associations broadly describe the area I have chosen to separate out as the third principal sense of brand equity, i.e. brand description. Aaker is quite right to include it as one of the dimensions on which a brand should be appraised; I have dealt with it separately because it seems to me essentially descriptive, rather than evaluative.

He is also right, I think, not to include price premium as a core *dimension* of brand equity, although he discusses it briefly (Aaker, 1991). I would agree that this is best seen as a measurable *output* of brand equity, rather than a part of brand equity itself (which raises another possible debate about what the phrase actually means). I start with it because it has nevertheless formed one of the most popular approaches to *measuring* brand equity.

## Price/demand measures (including modelling approaches)

One of the frequent benefits of a strong brand is its ability to command a higher price and/or less sensitivity to price increases than its competitors. It follows from this, that two dimensions on which the strength of a brand can be measured are its price premium, and its price elasticity. In other words, a brand is strong if people are prepared to pay more for it. Each of these can be measured in one of two ways: using market data or using experimental data.

### Price: using market data

Suppose we consider that an improvement in price premium while sustaining share (or improving share while sustaining price) is an improvement in brand equity. This has the merit of simplicity and needs no special research beyond reliable data on relative price and share, such as can be had from a good retail audit. The simplest way to imagine this is by plotting brand share and relative price on two axes of a graph. For each brand, we expect to see a relationship between price and share, popularly referred to as the 'demand curve'. 'Changing the shape of the demand curve'

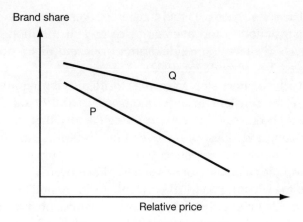

**Figure 3.1** Relationship between brand share and relative price.

or 'moving the demand curve to the right' have long been recognised as possible desired outcomes of advertising (Jones, 1986). This increase in demand could also be seen as an increase in the brand's equity.

In Figure 3.1 the Brand Q has a higher share than P when they both charge the same price premium over the market average, or can charge a higher price when they both have the same share. Also, Q loses less share than P when the price goes up; the slope of the line is less steep. These could be seen as two measures of Q's greater brand strength. If P and Q represent the same brand at different time periods, Q later than P, this could be taken as evidence of improved brand equity – caused, for instance, by advertising.

Price elasticity can also be estimated using econometric modelling; in the PG Tips case history (Grand Prix winner in the 1990 IPA Advertising Effectiveness Awards) there is an example of relative price elasticity quoted as evidence of brand strength/advertising effect (Feldwick, 1991).

A refinement of the price premium approach is offered by Longman-Moran Analytics in the USA (Moran, 1994). Here the definition of brand equity is: market share times relative price times a 'durability' factor. This last is an estimate of price elasticity based on market data. Crucial to this method (which makes it less easy than it sounds) is the importance of correctly defining the competitive set on which to base share and price differences, so that an apparently small brand may really need to be considered as a dominant niche player in a smaller category.

A further development of this approach is also to take distribution into account. Distribution and price are thus regarded as two 'contaminating' factors which disguise the 'real' underlying demand for competing brands. Simon Broadbent has developed a measure of consumer brand equity which he defines as: 'The sales share we would get, if we were at average price and had average distribution – and average price and distribution elasticities applied. Equity is, in effect, the residual after price and distribution effects have been allowed for.' (Broadbent, 1992).

It is conceptually a short step from this to identifying equity with the underlying 'base' or constant in an econometric model of sales or share. Broadbent has also been very active in exploring the idea that the constant in such equations can, and does, move over time, reflecting the underlying strength of a brand when all short-term factors – price, distribution, advertising, competitive activity or whatever – have been allowed for. This is referred to as the 'floating base' (Broadbent, 1993). A similar concept can be found in the modelling approach to brand equity measurement offered by The Consumer Affinity Company in the USA (Eubank, 1993).

The idea of searching for brand equity (brand strength) by factoring out all influences on market performance other than the brand name itself can lead into some complex procedures, such as that of Kamakura and Russell (1993). However, it is interesting that these American academic researchers validate their highly sophisticated approach by comparing results against a simple plotting of price premium versus brand share. In fact, this scatter plot approach remains one of the simplest and most practical ways to consider a brand's strength in the marketplace; for most purposes the use of 'multinomial logit models' to estimate something similar may be using a complicated sledgehammer to crack a fairly simple nut.

*Price: using experimental data*
Other approaches based on price take a different route. Instead of using market data, they use various forms of pricing research to estimate what share the brand would have at various different relative price levels. The equity measure is basically a calculation of the relative price at which each brand would have an equal share. (This is recognisable as the inversion of Broadbent's definition, given above.)

Joel Axelrod (1992) defines brand equity as 'the incremental amount your customer will pay to obtain your brand rather than a physically comparable product without your brand name'. In order to measure this, customers are divided into different cells and shown different combinations of the test brand and competitors at different price levels, and express preference using a constant sum technique.

Jim Crimmins of DDB (Crimmins, 1992) has a somewhat similar approach to measuring 'the amount of value added by a brand name' (to his credit, he avoids the dreaded E word). The interviewing approach sounds similar to Axelrod's. The output is an estimation of the price at which the test brand and each competitor are equally likely to be chosen. Notice that this measure of 'brand value added' is not absolute, but varies according to which competitor is taken as the comparison. Crimmins reports that the value added by the number one brand in a market averages 40% compared with store brands, but only averages 10% compared with the number two brand; in both cases there is a wide variation around this median figure.

Steve Roth (1991) describes the use of 'brand price trade-off' analysis to estimate brand equity. In this approach respondents choose their preferred brand at various different sets of price levels. By pooling all the respondents' individual decision processes the computer can simulate market outcomes at any set of prices. From a brand equity viewpoint, this micro modelling approach shows that a brand can have different 'equity' for different respondents.

As we shall see when looking at behavioural or attitudinal loyalty measures, any serious investigation into quantifying consumers' degree of 'attachment' to a brand is likely to discover this unsurprising truth – that some customers will be far more attached to the brand than others. It follows from this that figures which average all customers to provide a total brand score may be misleading. Conversely, the process of decomposing a brand's user base into more or less loyal users may be valuable in itself in planning marketing strategy. It may be that one of the main benefits of some brand equity research lies in this area, rather than the quest for a single yardstick for measuring brand strength.

Trade-off or conjoint approaches make it appear quite easy to separate brand name effects from other factors, which may make people forget that in real life separability is not always so clear cut. Can the Mercedes Benz name, for example, be separated from the reality of the Mercedes Benz car?

*Some general observations on price*
The attraction of using price as an indication of brand strength is that it relates closely to one of the main business benefits of branding. It is helpful in so far as it takes the focus off volume and adds the dimension of commanding a fair price for a trusted product.

However, there is more to brand strength than price premiums. There are strong brands which do not command a premium price, either because they are examples of 'scale economy branding' or because there is no directly substitutable product in the market. Mars bars would be an example of both. It is possible that relatively low price elasticity would still be an indication of brand strength, but if the policy of the manufacturer were to keep prices low – e.g. to keep competitors out of the market – this would be a somewhat hypothetical measure.

Another danger is a possible lag effect between price rises and share loss. It is a dangerous game to suppose that a brand can be made 'stronger' by increasing its price premium, but this could be one logical outcome of a system which measures brand equity in this way. The story of Marlboro in the period leading up to Marlboro Friday illustrates the risks (see Chapter 2).

This raises another question fundamental to defining what we mean by brand equity. Is it enough to consider a 'snapshot' of the brand's relative position at one point in time? Or are we really interested in its future potential for growth, its future resilience against attack? Price premiums may be a legacy of past strength (or present greed), more than they are a guarantee of future performance. Many brands in the UK grocery market might be seen as illustrating this uncertainty.

### Behavioural measures of brand loyalty

Brand loyalty, as mentioned before, is another expression whose meaning can vary. It is sometimes used, for instance, to describe the consumer's attitudinal orientation towards the brand (to be covered later). Its narrower sense, however, is based on records of actual purchasing behaviour as gathered in consumer panels.

One common method of using panel data to generate a measure of loyalty has been the concept of 'Share of Category Requirements', often referred to as Share of Requirements (SOR or SCR). The SOR for Nescafé is all Nescafé volume expressed as share of all instant coffee bought by respondents who bought Nescafé during the analysis period. This overall figure disguises a wide variation between individual buyers, some of whom will have bought no other coffee in the period (SOR = 100%), to those who bought it only once out of $n$ coffee purchases (SOR = $1/n*100\%$).

On this basis the more loyal customer is the one for whom the brand represents a higher share of category requirements; for instance, someone who buys seven jars of Nescafé in ten coffee purchasing occasions is more 'loyal' than someone who buys only three.

A good deal of attention has been paid to this behavioural definition of loyalty as an indicator of brand equity, especially in America. The idea is that the buyer with a higher share of category requirements is, obviously, far more important to the business (overall weight of purchase being equal) – also, implicitly, more emotionally attached to the brand and less willing to accept a substitute. (It does not, in fact, follow that this should always be the case and I am not sure what evidence exists for this assumption.) Therefore, if a brand's buyers show, overall, a higher average SOR, this could be seen as a sign of brand strength. (More usually, nowadays, the criterion is a higher proportion of buyers with an SOR above a certain level, rather than the average. Crimmins (1992) suggests the proportion of buyers with an SOR over 60%; Christiani (1993) argues for considering the whole distribution.)

Larry Light, a distinguished American researcher and Chairman of the Coalition for Brand Equity, uses the following example to demonstrate that brands with the same market shares can differ in loyalty as measured by SOR. He posits three imaginary brands: Brand A, which 100% of the user population buy 15% of the time; Brand B, which 15% buy 100% of the time; and Brand C, which half of the population buy 30% of the time. It will be seen that each of these brands has an identical 15% market share; but in terms of profitability, Brand B is claimed to be the most profitable (and the most secure?), and Brand A the least (Light, 1994).

The problem with this (admittedly hypothetical) example is that brands like A, B and C are not known to exist in normal markets. We have already observed that every brand shows a distribution of different loyalty levels ranging from 100% loyalists to those who bought the brand only once. Andrew Ehrenberg and his colleagues have shown repeatedly that over any time period this distribution tends to follow a standard pattern, which can be predicted within fairly narrow limits from three parameters. Two of these are market specific and can be estimated from knowing the category rate of purchase and the number of brands in the market; the third is simply the brand's market share. Hence any brand's average 'share of category requirements' can also be predicted, within narrow limits, from the same three parameters. Ehrenberg also shows that average 'share of requirements' actually varies little between brands in a market, though it is normally higher for brands with a larger share, an instance of the so-called 'double jeopardy' (Ehrenberg, 1988; Ehrenberg *et al.*, 1990; Ehrenberg & Scriven, 1995). Table 3.1 illustrates a typical finding.

There is an apparent conflict between Ehrenberg's findings (which have never been seriously disputed, though often ignored) and much American research based on SOR. The logic following from Ehrenberg's data is that brand strength measures based on share of category requirements are, once

**Table 3.1**  Market share and SOR.

| US instant coffee (annual) | Market share (%) | Share of category requirements (%) |
|---|---|---|
| Maxwell House | 19 | 39 |
| Sanka | 16 | 36 |
| Taster's Choice | 14 | 32 |
| High Point | 13 | 31 |
| All other brands | 12 | 32 |
| Folgers | 11 | 29 |
| Nescafé | 8 | 28 |
| Brim | 4 | 21 |
| Maxim | 3 | 23 |

Source: Ehrenberg & Scriven (1995)

again, mere tautologies for brand share; share of category requirements will only go up if brand share goes up, in which case, SOR may discriminate between consumers, but not usefully between brands.

An alternative to SOR as a way of defining loyalty is to look at patterns of purchasing over time, and use this to estimate the probability of each panel member buying the brand on the next purchase occasion. Alain Pioche (1992) of Nielsen describes such a system, and illustrates how it can be more sensitive than SOR by the following three purchasing sequences (A, B and C), where 1 = a purchase of the brand and 0 = purchase of another brand:

A:  1,1,1,1,1,0,0,0,0,0
B:  1,0,1,0,1,0,1,0,1,0
C:  0,0,0,0,0,1,1,1,1,1

The SOR here is identical for all three at 50%. On the basis that past buying is the best single predictor of future buying behaviour, Pioche estimates the probability of each respondent buying the brand next time as A = 0.21, B = 0.43, and C = 0.79. The results must be aggregated to create an overall measure for loyalty to a brand. This would then have the potential to vary continuously in time.

This idea has an intuitive appeal – it is like reading the form at a horse race. It may be thought, however, that at the aggregate level it will be unlikely to tell us anything new about the brand's health – if more people are buying the brand more often, this should be reflected in its overall brand share. However, what both SOR and this 'stochastic' approach show us is that any brand is bought by different groups of people, some very loyal (in behavioural terms), some not at all so. This mode of analysis is valuable in that it recognises that some customers are far more important to the brand than others, and that if these can be identified and targeted there can be significant improvements in marketing efficiency. This is the reverse of traditional 'conversion' models of marketing where the target was essentially conceived of as a non-user; it reflects a new and proper emphasis on the importance of the existing customer base (Hallberg, 1995).

Once the attempt is made to decompose the customer base in this way, a number of interlocking segmentations become possible which can make the process a complex one. Three common divisions are as follows:

(1)  Weight of category purchase. Here we should expect a wide distribution from heavy to very light users, where (at least) the 80:20 rule generally applies – a minority of buyers account for a majority of total category consumption.

(2) Share of category requirements (SOR) cuts across this, so that some of a brand's more loyal users will be heavy category users, and some very light. Ehrenberg points out that customers whose share of category requirements is 100% include a lot of very light users, as the easiest way to be classified as 100% loyal is to have only bought the category on a single occasion in the analysis period. This will also apply to others with a high SOR. Nevertheless, there will also be some heavy category users who are 80–100% loyal and these will account for a disproportionate volume of the business.

(3) In the United States, where deep price discounting has become a major force in packaged goods markets, there have been attempts to find general consumer segmentations that hold true across categories – so that some individuals are more brand loyal, some buy across a wide repertoire, and some are particularly likely to buy on deal (McQueen *et al.*, 1993). Discussion then arises over whether an occasional buyer of your brand is a more or less attractive prospect if he or she is a loyal buyer of a competing brand or a 'deal selective'.

All this may seem to be straying far away from our particular inquiry, and so in a way it is. However, the relevance of this to an overall measurement of brand equity is that a buyer whose 50% SOR is based on preference would constitute a greater brand asset than a buyer whose same SOR was based on deal buying. This suggests that analysis of buying patterns alone can be misleading unless it also includes some information about price.

Behavioural loyalty measures attempt to use consistency of behaviour as a proxy for attitude, or what we might call *commitment*. Given the influence of other factors such as inertia, availability and price, it is not obvious that this is entirely sound. Another way of looking at brand equity is to get a fix attitudinally on the number of buyers who are strongly committed to your brand, compared with the number who simply buy it because of price, because of habit or inertia, or just because it's the only one there. I describe some of these below.

### Attitudinal measures of brand loyalty

This section is concerned with general evaluative measures (affective or 'liking') more than with specific associations and beliefs about the brand (cognitive or 'thinking'), which belong more properly under the third main definition of brand equity as brand description.

The measures can take various forms, which need not be described here in detail: scales ranging from 'the only one I would ever consider' to 'I would never consider'; constant sum preference scales; brand 'for me' – 'not for me'. Any form of experimental price testing (such as those used by Axelrod (1992) or Crimmins (1992)) can be seen as a form of attitudinal research which takes claimed willingness to pay a price as its scale (hence it has been whimsically called 'dollarmetric scaling'). General measures of 'esteem' or 'quality' are intended to be sufficiently vague to cover all types of product or service, so they can be included under general affective measures.

In a way, such attitudinal measures take the most direct approach to the underlying concept that we want to measure – the relative preference, 'wantability' or attachment the consumer has for the brand, separated from 'external' factors such as price or distribution.

If brand attitudes are handled crudely on the 'eight out of ten cats prefer' basis or, worse still, as a single averaged figure, care needs to be taken – again – not to confound the *numbers* of a brand's devotees with the *degree* of their individual devotion to it. If this is done, then larger brands will tend to get the higher scores, and once again, we will learn nothing other than the fact they are big (Barwise & Ehrenberg, 1985). In fact, the use of preference and other measures to stand for brand equity has led to renewed interest in trying to understand how they represent different parts of the customer base by disaggregating them into groups (as in the analysis of loyalty, with which some researchers have tried to combine it).

One method of attitudinal segmentation is the conceptually very simple one proposed by Cramphorn (1992). This segments buyers of a brand into two groups, the discriminating and the undiscriminating, on the basis of a validated series of attitudinal statements. The percentage of discriminating buyers, plotted against brand share on the other axis, positions a brand as relatively stronger or weaker than others the same size.

A more complex attitudinal segmentation is Market Facts Inc.'s Conversion Model (Ceurvost, 1994). This segments buyers and non-buyers into four groups each: users are *entrenched*, *average*, *shallow* or *convertible*, while non-users can be *available*, *ambivalent*, *weakly unavailable* or *strongly unavailable*. It is claimed that trends in movements between these groups anticipate and predict market share movements; in particular, that as early as April 1991 the model predicted the decline in Marlboro share which led to Marboro Friday.

If this is true, it would imply that these questions are a major advance on the traditional 'intention to buy' question which was used for many years as a predictor of future behaviour. Bird and Ehrenberg (1966, 1967) showed many years ago, and Neil Barnard (1990) more recently, that claimed intention to buy reflects past behaviour much more than future behaviour. So a brand with a higher 'intention to buy' than its present brand share would imply is generally not, as you might expect, a brand that is about to grow, but a brand that is probably in decline. The number of respondents 'intending' to buy merely reflects the brand's past glories.

The proponents of the conversion model argue that behavioural loyalty alone can misrepresent consumers' level of emotional attachment to a brand, quoting evidence that many buyers with a high SOR have low emotional commitment. They also point out that in infrequent purchase choices, such as banks, cars or credit cards, SOR is not a practically useful concept (Ceurvost, 1994).

## Awareness/saliency measures

Brand awareness is one of Aaker's five dimensions of brand equity. He defines it as 'the ability to identify a brand as associated with a product category' – an important qualification. There is a difference between 'mere' awareness of a name, and associating it with a particular product. Being the first name to come to mind when thinking of coffee or hand drills or mouthwash is one indication that a brand 'owns' that particular category. Such associations can persist for a long time.

Brand awareness has a long pedigree as a desired outcome of marketing activity, deriving from the very earliest models of advertising effectiveness such as St Elmo Lewis' AIDA (Awareness – Interest – Desire – Action) in 1907. In most markets, recognition or a sense of familiarity with a brand name is considered a step towards improving acceptability and preference, other things being equal.

Awareness can be measured as recognition (prompted by the brand name), or spontaneous (prompted by some definition of the product field), with a further refinement in collecting the first name mentioned.

One well known general measure of brand equity, the Landor ImagePower study, consists of two measures: one is a simple measure of brand awareness, the other a more complex factor called 'esteem' (a general quality rating). The findings of this survey indicate that these two measures are substantially independent of each other, showing that brands that are well known or easily called to mind are not always highly thought of or likely to be preferred (although more so in America than in Europe) (Owen, 1993).

Another major cross-category survey of relative brand strength, the Young & Rubicam Brand Asset Valuator (Young & Rubicam, 1994), includes familiarity as one of four key dimensions of brand strength (the others being esteem, relevance and differentiation). Even here they are careful to point out that their definition of 'familiarity' embraces more than mere name awareness.

In fact it is generally true that high levels of awareness are created by a brand's size, ubiquity, and/or scale of promotional activity, while they tell us relatively little about the brand's 'strength' in the sense of the consumer's attachment to it or preference for it. Such measures tend to favour brands that are relatively or absolutely large, so that once more we are in danger of confounding size with strength.

## Sense 3. Brand equity = brand description: descriptive associations/attributes of the brand

Some researchers talk about the collection of brand image data, positioning mapping and the like as if this is brand equity. David Aaker includes this as one of his dimensions of brand equity. It is widely assumed that the associations or attributes which a brand acquires are the main creators of the brand's strength, as when Alex Biel argues that 'brand image drives brand equity' (Biel, 1992).

A wide variety of techniques, qualitative and quantitative, exist for eliciting consumers' associations with and perceptions of a brand, by inviting the respondent to link each brand with words or pictures, or to position them relative to each other in multidimensional scaling. There is no need to describe them all here.

More relevant to the brand equity debate are attempts to relate these kinds of data, which are essentially descriptive, to dimensions of attitudinal or behavioural loyalty, i.e. brand strength, as described above. It is through this linkage that what we might call brand image data has attached itself to the brand equity concept, in procedures which are often known in the USA as 'brand equity modelling'.

Attempts to model general affective attitudes to brands in this way can follow two main approaches, which I shall call cross-sectional or time series. *Cross-sectional* is to look for correlations between the individuals in the sample – so that if the strongest preferrers show a strong tendency to rate the brand on attribute Y, the inference is that associating the brand with attribute Y creates preference. This procedure is not new; it goes back to the St James model of the 1960s, and the objection made against it at the time, that it is impossible to distinguish cause and effect in such correlations, is still a matter for debate. *Time series analysis* requires a set of such data over time from a tracking study; if a sudden decline in one particular attribute happens at the same time as a decline in general favourability scores, that attribute is assumed to be an important 'driver'. Both approaches can be and often are combined with the loyalty segmentations described, so that the 'drivers' for each brand's loyalists or rejectors (including competitive brands) can be computed. All these procedures are controversial, but undeniably attractive for many reasons that go beyond the measurement aspect of brand equity;

they offer guidance for advertising and marketing strategy, and an appearance, at least, of controlling complexity: 'If we can improve *this* image dimension for *these* people, our brand equity – and profit – will go up *this* much'. In their favour it must be said that they grapple with the complexity of a real user base, where different individuals vary. Not everyone will be convinced that they deliver all they promise.

## What's good about the 'brand equity movement?'

Before moving on to some more critical conclusions, I would suggest that the new focus on brand equity indicates a desirable paradigm shift in marketing thinking. (This would be especially true in the USA.) The key elements of this paradigm shift would be:

- A focus on the value of *keeping* present customers, as against converting new ones.
- A recognition that marketing should be about selling at the right *price*, not just shifting volumes.
- A focus on protecting and developing a *long-term profit stream*, not just getting the next sale.
- An understanding that brands survive and prosper only if they keep their *'contract'* with the customer.
- A revival of interest in the concepts of brand *differentiation* and *positioning*.

However, the idea that all this is somehow explained by the motions and dimensions of a mysterious substance called brand equity is much harder to defend.

## Dispelling the brand equity myths

### Brand value isn't the same as brand strength

I have argued throughout this chapter that financial valuation of a brand as a separable asset is fundamentally different from the concept of measuring a brand's 'strength' relative to the consumer. Calling the two things by the same name is confusing, even misleading. While the two concepts each have some kind of validity as ideas, the connection between them is a very tenuous one. Valuation is essentially a forecast, and therefore can be volatile and dependent on variable assumptions. A measure of brand strength, on the other hand, ought to reflect some kind of objective reality, and should therefore be reasonably stable and replicable. One represents the future, the other represents the present. And present brand strength is only one factor – not necessarily an important one – in constructing a future forecast. Barwise (1993) points out that none of the short-term measures of brand loyalty has yet been shown to have any long-term predictive power.

It should follow from this that the idea of using brand valuation as a yardstick for evaluating and rewarding management is a dangerous one. Why pay a brand manager a bonus for something his successors may or may not succeed in doing in future years?

### There is no single number that represents brand strength

It should at least be clear that whatever the different measures of brand strength represent, they are not all measuring the same thing.

A brand's ability to command a price premium is different from its SOR (the brand leader may have 40% more 'equity' than the store brand measured as price premium, but the same or even less SOR among its buyers).

Loyalty as shown by probability models is different from attitudinal measures (Pioche, 1992), and also, as mentioned, different from SOR.

Different price measures give quite different results (e.g. Crimmins (1992) explicitly points out that his measure of brand value is not the same as the price premium in the market).

Ceurvost (1994) states that the Conversion model's measure of 'commitment' is not related to SOR.

To talk about a brand's 'strength or 'health' is after all a metaphor. We use such metaphors all the time (as when we speak of the sun 'rising') but shouldn't confuse them with science. We seem to have got so used to the metaphor of 'brand as person' that we have to remind ourselves it isn't literally true!

What we mean when we say a brand is 'strong' is really something like 'the main performance indicators look positive'. There may be many different performance indicators, and the ones that matter may vary from brand to brand and from time to time. No sensible person would expect to represent the health of an individual, or of a nation's economy, by a single figure (and the results of such a mistake, if made, could be disastrous); so it is with brands.

### It's difficult to separate brand strength from brand size

Another theme in this chapter is that many of the performance indicators discussed tend to be largely a function of a brand's sales in the market. Some key performance indicators are, indeed, sales based (as in the price/share charts). Attitudinal and awareness measures relate largely to brand size, and even SOR has been shown to be predictable from it.

However, this does not entirely justify Ehrenberg's apparent view (if I understand him correctly) that brand strength and brand size are exactly the same, so that the first term is completely redundant. It is easy to imagine situations where research shows a degree of consumer demand for a brand not reflected in sales, or where sales are inflated by factors other than consumer demand. These would be very valuable situations for a brand manager to know about, the one representing an opportunity and the other a threat. It is the object of 'brand monitors' and other attitudinal research to provide information like this, but providers and users of such data need to be aware of the pitfalls involved.

## What do we really want to measure?

What we have really been discussing is not the elusive 'brand equity', but a variety of different performance measures and forecasting techniques. Instead of the essentialist mistake (invent a thing called 'brand equity' and find ways to measure it), we should decide what we want to measure (and, if necessary, find names for each of these things). The main things a brand manager or brand owner might want to measure, then, will be as follows:

### Current performance

How well is the brand doing now, relative to competitors, or to previous years? Indicators would include share/price combinations, and modelling techniques that attempt to separate underlying consumer demand from external factors such as distribution (a simple version of this, of course, being rate of sale).

### Diagnosis of current trends, and 'early warning systems'

This is where the various consumer measures of attitudes, awareness, and buying behaviour come into their own – as long as we remember that these data are usually to a large extent reflecting sales performance. They are also extremely valuable in decomposing aggregate sales patterns into different consumer groups. More perceptual measures, such as surveys of a brand's relative positioning or differentiation, are relevant here too.

### The brand's chances of future, long-term profitability

The real goal for brand owners is to achieve what Larry Light has called *enduring, profitable growth*. This brings us to the heart of what the various attempts to measure brand equity are trying to do. Current performance indicators can show short-term increases in sales (e.g. by promoting), or in profit (e.g. by increasing price), or even, occasionally, both (by promoting while reducing quality or investment), while at the same time the chances of the brand succeeding in the future are being reduced by the same actions. It *would* be a good thing if we had a performance indicator that rewarded brand management for protecting the long-term health of the brand, rather than merely maximising its share or profit in the current year. However, it is not clear that such an indicator has yet been found, or even whether it is possible for one to exist. Certainly many of the simple measures put forward as representing 'brand equity', such as relative demand, do not by themselves fit the bill as has already been argued. Conceptually, the problem is the same as with brand valuation for financial purposes – what we are looking for is an estimate of how the brand *will* perform some years into the future. While this may be something that management should form a judgement about, we have no objective way of capitalising current investments in a brand's future. What we can be alert to are improvements in current performance that are merely a result of manipulating price or investment, and we can make a judgement – it can hardly be put more strongly than this – on whether these changes in policy are likely to maintain the brand's competitive position into the future. This returns us, in fact, to considering current performance and diagnosing the reasons for current performance.

### An overall valuation

For buying, selling, valuing a brand, or as an aid to future strategic planning, an overall valuation can be attempted. There are various ways of tackling this tricky job, but they all tend to be essentially forecasts of future performance (translated into net present value). Such forecasts involve competitive and strategic judgements, and other considerations such as legal ownership, as well as current performance measures.

### Brand extendability

Another factor that an owner might want to measure (but which is only briefly discussed in the present chapter) is *brand extendability*: how could a brand's reputation be used in other product fields? Although quite a lot of academic work has been done in this area, it is not obvious that any really useful principles have been discovered. Consumer research might be of some use in making this kind of decision. From a valuation point of view, to include hypothetical performance of a brand in a different category is about as speculative as you can get. It is, surely, part of the great brand equity myth that 'a strong brand' can stroll with ease and impunity into neighbouring territories and clean up. Experience tends to show rather the contrary.

## Final conclusions

We need to manage brands with a view to their long-term market position, respecting their contract and relationship with the consumer. There are many different kinds of performance indicator which will monitor these factors. We can also put a value on brands as assets when necessary, and buy and sell them, but we can do all this without assuming the existence of anything called brand equity. In fact we might find the whole area easier to understand if people stopped using those words altogether.

## References

Aaker, D. (1991) *Managing Brand Equity: Capitalizing on the Value of a Brand Name*. The Free Press, New York.

Ambler, T. & Styles, C. (1995) Brand equity: towards measures that matter. Pan'agra Working Paper No. 95-902, London Business School.

Axelrod, J.N. (1992) The use of experimental design in monitoring brand equity. Paper given at ESOMAR seminar 'The Challenge of Branding Today and in the Future?', Brussels, October, pp. 13–26.

Barnard, N. (1990) What can you do with tracking studies and what are their limitations? *Admap*, April, p. 23.

Barrett, H. & Bertolotti, N.P. (1992) Brand evaluation. Paper given at ESOMAR seminar 'The Challenge of Branding Today and in the Future?', Brussels, October, pp. 1–12.

Barwise, P. (1993) Brand equity, snark or boojum? *International Journal of Research in Marketing* 10(1), pp. 93–104.

Barwise, P. & Ehrenberg, A.S.C. (1985) Consumer beliefs and brand usage. *Journal of the Market Research Society* 27(2), pp. 81–93.

Barwise, P., Higson, C., Likierman, A. & Marsh, P. (1989) *Accounting for Brands*. London Business School/Institute of Chartered Accountants, London.

Barwise, P. & Robertson, T. (1992) Brand portfolios. *European Management Journal* 10(3), pp. 277–285.

Biel, A.L. (1992) How brand image drives brand equity. ARF Workshop, New York, February. In *Exploring Brand Equity* (Christiani, A., Donius, J.F., Lockwood, T.C. & Moran, W.T., eds, 1995), pp. 9–24. Advertising Research Foundation, New York.

Biel, A.L. (1993) Converting image into equity. In *Brand Equity and Advertising* (Aaker, D. & Biel, A.L., eds), p. 67. Lawrence Erlbaum Associates, Hillsdale, New Jersey.

Bird, M. & Ehrenberg, A.S.C. (1966, 1967) Intentions to buy and claimed brand usage. *Operational Research Quarterly* 17, pp. 27–46 and 18, pp. 65–66.

Broadbent, S. (1992) Using data better – a new approach to sales analyses. *Admap*, January, pp. 48–54.

Broadbent, S. (1993) Advertising effects: more than short term. *Journal of the Market Research Society* 35(1), pp. 37–49.

Ceurvost, R.W. (1994) A brand equity measure based on consumer commitment to brands. ARF Brand Equity Workshop, New York, February. In *Exploring Brand Equity* (Christiani, A., Donius, J.F., Lockwood, T.C. & Moran, W.T., eds, 1995), pp. 65–84. Advertising Research Foundation, New York.

Christiani, A. (1993) Measuring and monitoring brand loyalty and its role in managing brand equity. ARF Research Day, New York, October. In *Exploring Brand Equity* (Christiani, A., Donius, J.F., Lockwood, T.C. & Moran, W.T., eds, 1995), pp. 125–136. Advertising Research Foundation, New York.

Cowley, D. (ed.) (1989) *Understanding Brands*. Kogan Page/Account Planning Group, London.

Cramphorn, M.F. (1992) Are there bounds on brand equity? Paper given at ESOMAR seminar 'The Challenge of Branding Today and in the Future?', Brussels, October, pp. 41–54.

Crimmins, J.C. (1992) Better measurement and management of brand value. *Journal of Advertising Research* 32(4), pp. 11–19.

Ehrenberg, A.S.C. (1988) *Repeat Buying*. Revised edition. Charles Griffin & Company, London; OUP, New York.

Ehrenberg, A.S.C. (1993) If you're so strong, why aren't you bigger? Making the case against brand equity. *Admap*, October, pp 13–14. (See also *Admap*, December 1993 for comments by Ambler and Feldwick and Ehrenberg's reply.)

Ehrenberg, A.S.C., Goodhardt, G.J. & Barwise, T.P. (1990) Double jeopardy revisited. *Journal of Marketing* 54, July, pp. 82–91.

Ehrenberg, A.S.C. & Scriven, J. (1995) Added values or propensities to buy. JOAB Report 1, South Bank Business School, London.

Eubank, S.K. (1993) Understanding brand equity: a volumetric model. ARF Brand Equity Research Day, New York, October. In *Exploring Brand Equity* (Christiani, A., Donius, J.F., Lockwood, T.C. & Moran, W.T., eds, 1995), pp 319–329. Advertising Research Foundation, New York.

Feldwick, P. (ed.) (1991) *Advertising Works 6*. NTC Publications, Henley-on-Thames.

Gardner, B.B. & Levy, S.J. (1955) The product and the brand. *Harvard Business Review*, March/April, pp. 33–39.

Hallberg, G. (1995) *All Consumers Are Not Created Equal*. John Wiley & Sons, New York.

Jones, J.P. (1986) *What's in a Name: Advertising and the Concept of Brands*. Lexington Books, Lexington, Massachusetts.

Jones, J.P. (1991) Over-promise and under-delivery. Paper given at ESOMAR seminar 'What do we know about how advertising works and how promotions work?', Amsterdam, April, pp. 13–27.

Kamakura, W.A & Russell, G.J. (1993) Measuring brand value with scanner data. *International Journal of Research in Marketing* 10(1), pp. 9–22.

Kapferer, J.-N. (1992) *Strategic Brand Management: New Approaches to Creating and Evaluating Brand Equity*. Kogan Page, London. Translated from Kapferer, J.-N. (1991) *Les Marques, Capital de l'Entreprise*. Les Editions D'Organisation, Paris.

King, S. (1970) *What is a Brand?* J. Walter Thompson, London.

Light, L. (1994) *The Fourth Wave: Brand Loyalty Marketing*. Coalition for Brand Equity, New York.

Lockwood, T.C. (1994) The confessions of a brand equity junkie. ARF Annual Conference. In *Exploring Brand Equity* (Christiani, A., Donius, J.F., Lockwood, T.C. & Moran, W.T., eds, 1995). Advertising Research Foundation, New York.

McQueen, J., Foley, C. & Deighton, J. (1993) Decomposing a brand's consumer franchise into buyer types. In *Brand Equity and Advertising* (Aaker, D. & Biel, A.L., eds), pp. 235–246. Lawrence Erlbaum Associates, Hillsdale, New Jersey.

McWilliam, G. (1993) A tale of two gurus. *International Journal of Research in Marketing* 10(1), pp, 105–111.

Moran, W.T. (1994) Brand equity: the durability of brand value. ARF Brand Equity Workshop, New York, February. In *Exploring Brand Equity* (Christiani, A., Donius, J.F., Lockwood, T.C. & Moran, W.T., eds, 1995), pp. 293–318. Advertising Research Foundation, New York.

Murphy, J. (1990) Assessing the value of brands. *Long Range Planning* 23(3), pp. 23–29.

Owen, S. (1993) The Landor image power survey: a global assessment of brand strength. In *Brand Equity and Advertising* (Aaker, D. & Biel, A.L., eds), pp. 11–30. Lawrence Erlbaum Associates, Hillsdale, New Jersey.

Pioche, A. (1992) A definition of brand equity relying on attitudes and validated by behaviour. Paper given at ESOMAR seminar 'The Challenge of Branding Today and in the Future?', Brussels, October, pp. 27–40.

Reeves, R. (1961) *Reality in Advertising*. Alfred A. Knopf, New York.

Roth, S. (1991) Pricing, profits and equity. Third ARF Advertising and Promotions Workshop, New York, February. In *Exploring Brand Equity* (Christiani, A., Donius, J.F., Lockwood, T.C. & Moran, W.T., eds, 1995), pp 175–188. Advertising Research Foundation, New York.

Taylor, J.A. (1992) Brand equity: its meaning, measurement and management. Paper given at ESOMAR seminar 'The Challenge of Branding Today and in the Future?', Brussels, October, pp. 55–75.

Young & Rubicam (1994) *Brand Asset Valuator Prospectus*. Young & Rubicam, New York.

## Afterword

Whatever happened to 'brands on the balance sheet'? When RHM pioneered the practice in 1988 it started an energetic debate among accountants. Some argued that a balance sheet should be a historical record of actual transactions, while others wanted it to represent the current value of the business. The dispute was resolved in December 1997 when the UK Accounting Standards Board (ASB) published Financial Reporting Standard 10 (FRS 10) on 'goodwill and intangible assets'. This ruled that acquired brands *must* be included in the balance sheet at their actual acquisition cost (previously they would have been written off as 'goodwill'), but that internally created brand value *must not* be included in balance sheets.

FRS 10 means it is no longer possible even to consider balance sheet valuations as a monitor of marketing success. On the other hand, the ASB has helped in a way by separating the question of how best to value brands from the strict requirements of financial reporting. Putting brand value on the balance sheet encouraged a tacit assumption that a brand's value can be objective and absolute. However, as I argued in this chapter, it is not, and this point has also been made, in greater depth, by Tim Ambler of the London Business School (Ambler, 2000, pp. 46–48), who defines brand equity as 'the storehouse of *future* profits that results from *past* marketing activities'. I rather like this definition – it makes it clear that brand equity is something real, but also that to put a value on it is no more objective that putting a *value* on the next five years' profits.

Having said that, financial reporting is not the same as financial planning, and estimating future cash flows, however tricky that may be, is what financial analysts do all the time. Future net cash flows, discounted by the cost of capital, are what create shareholder value. One other development since this chapter was written is the growing popularity of shareholder value analysis (SVA) as a management concept, and the increasing recognition that brands – through the loyalty they engender, their resistance to competition, their ability to charge a premium – are powerful engines for the sustainable cash flows that create shareholder value. SVA can also show vividly how continued investment in marketing, while it generally makes a brand less profitable in short-term profit and loss, is very likely to lead to increased shareholder value in a longer-term view (Doyle, 2000). It is this kind of analysis, rather than the notion of 'brands on the balance sheet', that promises to lead to more productive cooperation in future between marketing and finance.

### References
Ambler, T. (2000) *Marketing and the Bottom Line*. FT/Prentice Hall, London.
Doyle, P. (2000) *Value Based Marketing*. John Wiley & Sons, Chichester.

Chapter 4

# How Should You Research Brands?

## What brands are, and how they work

Oreo, Tampax, Citibank, Daewoo, Danone, Brentano's, Knorr, Tesco, Harley-Davidson, Faber, Kwikfit, Président, Guinness... nearly everywhere, and in nearly all categories, our buying and selling is organised around brand names and brand symbols. Not just the Marlboros and the Coca-Colas, but hundreds of small and local names mediate consumer choices. In fact, it is harder to think of marketplaces where brands don't exist than where they do – buying vegetables in a street market might be one, though even here regular buyers may come to favour one stall over another, or look out for fruit with a certain label of origin.

Even in situations where brands don't exist, consumers invent them where they can. It is said that in the Soviet Union people distinguished between tyres from different factories, on the evidence of serial numbers printed in the rubber, and came to associate the 'brands' with different levels of quality and reliability.

This story begins to indicate how brands work, and why the brand has become such a central concept in marketing. The brand name, or mark, is at its simplest a *badge of origin*. In most societies this identification is protected by trade mark law. The buyers of goods or services develop associations with the mark which help them make their purchase decisions. Some brands will

Originally published as 'Researching brands', in *ESOMAR Handbook of Market and Social Research* (C. McDonald & P. Vangelder, eds), 1997.
Copyright © ESOMAR® 2001.
Permission for using this material has been granted by ESOMAR®, Amsterdam, the Netherlands.
For further information, please refer to the ESOMAR website: www.esomar.nl.

be associated with consistent quality, some less so. They may be associated with specific performance benefits, cleaning power or good taste. A brand thus offers *reassurance*, which not only helps the buyer make a safe decision, but actually adds value by creating good feelings of security and anticipation. Without brands, every purchase would be a gamble.

More than this: brands become part of the network of *symbols* with which we structure our lives and our relationships. Brands become associated with certain types of people, with certain occasions or emotional values. We choose one brand over another, to make a statement to others, and to make a statement to ourselves. All these meanings that brands take on have implications for business, and it is in the interests of the brand owner to control them as much as possible.

What creates and modifies the meaning of a brand for those who come into contact with it? Product or service quality is clearly very important. But it is by no means everything. Our perceptions can be powerfully 'framed' by what we are told about a brand, and by the visual codes in which it is packaged. As many products are, objectively, almost impossible to tell apart in normal use, these 'framings' may become the deciding factor as long as product quality keeps up to a basic expectation. Consequently, activities such as packaging and advertising become of great importance; they create, maintain or change perceptions and expectations of the brand in the consumer's mind. In the words of Al Ries and Jack Trout (1993),

> 'There is no objective reality. There are no facts. There are no best products. All that exists in the world of marketing are perceptions in the mind of the customer or prospect. The perception is the reality. Everything else is an illusion.'

Success breeds success (or the reverse). A brand that someone has known and used for years can maintain its good reputation, despite a falling off in actual performance. Things may have to get seriously bad before the user of such a brand is forced to revalue it. Likewise, if everybody else appears to continue using the brand happily, I have to be quite strongly convinced before I disagree with them. We are all creatures of habit and conformity, and established brands derive great benefit from this.

## The business value of brands

Most companies, if you push them into a statement of their overall business objective, will come up with something like 'long-term profitable growth'. In other words, their owners and stockholders are not just interested in this year's profits, but in a secure expectation that those profits will continue, and grow, for a number of years to come. An established and successful brand name is one of the best machines for delivering this long-term profit stream. Sales that are not associated with a strong brand (e.g. supplying a retailer's own brand) are relatively vulnerable to competitors, to innovation, to price wars. But a strong relationship between the brand and its end-consumers is not so easily disrupted, although eventually it can be eroded.

That is why brand names are often bought and sold for considerable sums of money – prices which reflect, not the tangible assets of the brand, the bricks and mortar and machinery, which are usually pretty small, but the expectation of continuing the brand's level of sales into the foreseeable future. This prospect is associated with the brand name and its meaning to the public.

It is not, of course, guaranteed. A brand name is not an annuity and those who imagine it is often come unstuck. No brand is so strong that it cannot be seriously challenged by environmental change or by determined competition, and even the best brand can be destroyed extremely rapidly by inspired mismanagement. However, within certain limits, it is a sound bet that a brand's sales will continue well into the future, and this is why brand names are worth money.

## Implications of the brand concept for marketing, and the need for measurement

Suppose, then, we redefine the core task of marketing to 'managing the relationship between the brand and the consumer'. This doesn't exclude sales – buying the brand is a key component of the relationship we want to have! However, it goes *beyond* sales as well. There may be things we would do to make an immediate sale which would, at the same time, influence the longer-term relationship adversely. There might be other things that would improve short-term profitability, such as reducing the quality of the product or cutting the advertising, which would also risk damaging the relationship as perceived by the consumer. In other words, there may be a trade-off between a short-term focus – on sales, especially volume sales, or on profit – and on the longer-term prospect as it depends on the consumer's relationship with the brand.

Nevertheless, management demands measurement. Volumes and profits are measured in hard numbers and generally have hard targets to meet. If 'the brand relationship' is to be set alongside these as a goal for management, it also needs to be defined in terms which we can measure. Thus in recent years we have seen an increased demand for ways in which the brand relationship, or 'brand strength', can be measured, and a corresponding range of proposals from researchers, consultants, and ad agencies as to how it might be done.

These are some of the questions a manager might want answers to:

- Is my brand stronger or weaker than it was last year?
- Is it stronger or weaker than specific competitors?
- Which are the strongest brands in my portfolio?
- In which geographical markets is my brand strongest or weakest?
- How does my brand measure up against brands in other categories?
- How much is my brand worth in financial terms?

They sound reasonable questions, but they are by no means straightforward ones. The difficulty lies in the ambiguity of the word 'strong'. We talk of 'strong brands' and generally assume we all know what we mean, but the discipline of turning this concept into something measurable indicates that the expression can have a number of shades of meaning. We might say a brand is strong because it is a dominant brand leader; or because it is highly thought of by its users; or because we believe it has great potential; or because we are confident in its future ability to generate profit in the longer term; or we might explain it in numerous other ways. Although there is some tendency for brands that would score well on some definitions of strength to also do well on others, it is by no means necessary that they should. All these definitions are different and potentially independent of each other.

We should recognise at the outset, then, that there is no single dimension on which we could all agree to define 'brand strength'. What we can do is understand the nature of a brand's relationship with its public on a number of different dimensions, and on these dimensions we can quantify trends and compare it with other brands in its own category, and in some cases with brands in other categories. We can, if we wish, create a single measure to represent our overall estimation of brand strength, but this will necessarily be a somewhat artificial and arbitrary concept, like indices of 'standard of living' or 'national prosperity' used by economists – like these, such a measure might have its uses but we should not forget its limitations.

We can divide the various approaches to measuring brand strength into three classes:

(1) Those based on observation of how the brand is currently performing in the marketplace.
(2) Those based on attempts to access the relevant beliefs, associations and attitudes that are in consumers' minds.
(3) Those based on attempts to estimate the brand's future performance and profit streams, and thus put a financial value on the brand as a corporate asset.

## Definitions of brand strength based on market performance

Discussions of 'brand strength' or 'equity' sometimes suggest that these are abstract values, somehow quite separate from the brand's actual sales in the marketplace. Certainly we are assuming there are aspects of the brand's 'strength' that may not be apparent just be looking at its marketplace performance (and hope to show as we go on that this assumption is correct). However, this should not blind us to the fact that the most obvious evidence of a brand's relationship with its public is normally to be found in its sales, and a brand that is struggling in the marketplace can only be said to be 'strong' – if at all – in specific and limited ways. This is underlined by the fact that most forms of financial brand valuation, whether for sales or balance sheet purposes, start by looking at the brand's current sales and profit.

In one sense it is always true to say that a big, successful brand is a strong brand, but only in the tautological sense that we have made size and success our definition of strength. And this does not really help very much in addressing the management needs we explained earlier. What we are interested in is interpreting sales data so that they may tell us something extra about the brand's strength in a way that is not merely tautological.

The main possibility here is to define brand strength as the strength of consumer demand for our brand, relative to its competitors. 'Demand' and 'sales' will normally march in step, but not necessarily. In order to disentangle the two, we need to look at the data with particular care. In other words, we need to make some allowance for factors that might be influencing aspects of sales without actually improving consumer demand. The most important ones are *price* and *distribution*.

In most competitive markets, the biggest single influence on short-term movements in volume share is relative price. 'Demand', in economic terms, is shown by the amount of a product that will be sold at a given price. If the price is reduced, it is likely that more will be sold, but this need not represent an increase in demand. We can apply the same principles when analysing the movements in share in a consumer market.

In Figure 4.1 Brand A has increased its share year on year, but has also cut its price. Its 'demand curve' is unchanged; we conclude that consumers do not rate the brand more highly than they did, but buy more of it because it is cheaper. Brand B, on the other hand, has increased its price and its sales have declined. But as with A, both points lie on the same curve. Although it appears to be doing badly, in consumer demand terms it has remained unchanged. Brand C, however, has increased its price and maintained the same brand share. We interpret this as a real increase in consumer strength for the brand.

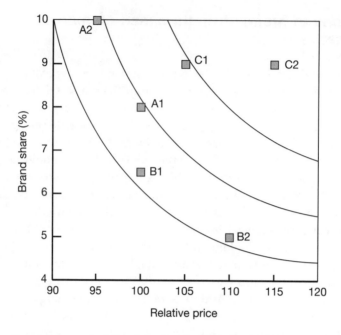

**Figure 4.1**   Brand share and relative price for brands A, B and C in years 1 and 2.

The other factor that can misrepresent consumer standing of a brand is distribution. Brand Q sells three times as much as Brand R: but R is only available in 30% of the trade, and Q is in 90%. If we calculate a 'rate of sale' by dividing each brand's sales by its percentage distribution, we can see that they are very similar. Such an analysis tells us that R has a trade problem, not a consumer problem; it suggests an opportunity for the brand as this can be overcome.

Such analyses may seem very simple – they are certainly not new – but they should not be overlooked. They can in themselves tell us a good deal about the overall consumer strength of a brand and how it is changing relative to competition. They may also raise issues that can be explored further through the other dimensions that we can measure from survey research.

As well as looking at price and distribution separately, they can be combined to examine movements in rate of sale against movements in relative price. From here it is a short step to creating econometric models of market share which can take other factors, such as advertising and promotion, into account. In some circumstances we might want to consider these or other factors as short-term influences that obscure a longer-term trend in consumer demand.

Share models generally take the form of an equation $S = K + aD + bP + c$
$X...$, where $S$ is share; $D$, $P$, $X$, etc. are explanatory variables (distribution,
price, other); $a$, $b$, $c$ are parameters; and $K$ is a constant (see page 119 for a
fuller explanation). There is a case for saying that $K$ represents some underlying level of consumer demand, equivalent to what the share would be
without advertising or promotion and at a parity level of price and distribution. Despite the formal assumption that this base is a constant, there is much
evidence from modelling work that it moves over time – this has been one
promising approach to quantifying the elusive 'longer-term effects' of advertising. Conceptually this is a logical development of what we have been
talking about. (For all these types of analysis, see Broadbent, 1990, 1992.)

### Focus on price

In the example above we interpreted a brand's ability to increase its price
premium without losing corresponding volume share as an overall
improvement in the brand's consumer strength. And indeed, the ability to
charge a higher price and thus maintain better margins is often cited as one
of the major benefits of being a 'strong brand'.

Some researchers have suggested that the price premium itself can be
interpreted as an indicator of brand strength. Others have developed
measures of brand strength which are based on versions of 'brand price
trade-off analysis' – estimating in a laboratory situation how much extra
consumers are prepare to pay for a brand (Axelrod, 1992; Crimmins, 1992).

This is an appealing line of argument and in some cases such measures
may be revealing, but price premium does not universally equate to brand
strength. Brands that do not choose to sell at a premium price can have
powerful consumer relationships – sometimes the very strength of the
relationship is based on a consistently low or affordable price promise.

There is also a dangerous line of thought that goes like this, 'Strong brands
charge higher prices. So to strengthen our brand, we'll put the price up!'
Higher prices may improve short-term profitability, and so impact on a
brand's financial value, but they may also jeopardise the relationship with
the consumer, especially if repeated too often. If customers feel the brand is
taking advantage of their loyalty, they may reject the brand altogether.

In the late 1980s and early 1990s Marlboro, the leading cigarette brand in
the United States, took annual price increases of up to 10% – well ahead of
inflation. By 1992 the brand was losing share at around 0.5% each month, as
more and more retailer brands took advantage of Marlboro's high pricing to
undercut them, sometimes by half. In April, the management took the drastic
decision to cut Marlboro's price by 20%, an event which the *Wall Street
Journal* hailed as the 'death of brands' and which triggered a collapse in stock

prices, not just for Marlboro's owners Philip Morris but for many other strongly branded companies (see Chapter 2).

*Financial World*, which had in 1992 valued the Marlboro brand at \$51.6 billion, revalued it after 'Marlboro Friday' at \$33 billion – a huge change. And yet, ironically, Marlboro's consumer relationship was probably *stronger* after the price cut than it had been before. This illustrates that a high price tag doesn't always tell the whole story about how a brand stands with its customers. It also shows us how financial valuations of brands, whatever their uses, are not identical to measures of consumer brand strength – a point we will return to towards the end of this chapter.

A more subtle way of using price to estimate a brand's consumer strength is to look not at its premium, but its *price elasticity* – the amount by which its sales will rise or fall as a result of a 1% price cut or increase. Such elasticities can be derived from econometric modelling (and thus another example of looking at marketplace performance for an indication of brand strength). An example of this is given in the IPA Grand Prix winning paper on PG Tips (Cooper *et al.*, 1991).

## Definitions of brand strength based on 'what's in people's minds'

Our original explanation of the whole branding phenomenon put great emphasis on the meanings and associations that a brand can create in the mind of the consumer. So the obvious place to anatomise the strength of a brand should be the consumer's mind.

David Aaker (1995) visualises each brand name as a box in the consumer's brain, in which are stored away all the bits of information and associations to do with that brand. The whole box is then in turn filed away under 'positive' or 'negative' feelings. This is as good an image as any, although like all metaphors for how the mind works it is likely to be too simplistic and therefore runs the risk of sometimes being misleading. It will serve however to introduce three basic categories that we can use to try and gather information about what goes on in the consumer's mind:

(1) Awareness – whether there is a box for our brand there at all, or whether it is easy to find.
(2) Associations and beliefs – what's in the box. This is a big area in itself with many dimensions to it. (You could imagine smaller boxes inside this box, except that would be too neat and tidy – perhaps we can think of some boxes, some paper bags, some loose items, some broken bits and a couple of bottles that have leaked.)

(3) Attitude – how the consumer feels about the brand, positive, negative or indifferent.

Each of these areas can be interpreted to tell us about an aspect of a brand's 'strength'. You could say a brand is strong because many people have heard of it or spontaneously think of it; you could certainly say it is strong if many people express great loyalty or affection for it, in their words or in their actions. In between, a brand can be called strong if it is strongly associated with imagery or functional benefits that we interpret as desirable for consumers.

### Awareness

'Brand awareness' can be defined in a number of different ways. There is what is commonly called prompted awareness, but which might more simply be called recognition – asking respondents 'Which of these brand names have you heard of?' This can be qualified in various ways, such as specifying a particular category ('Which of these brands of sausages have you heard of?'); you can also sometimes get different results if you show a pack or logo rather than just the name. It's possible to develop a scale of familiarity.

Then there is spontaneous awareness, where the respondent has to volunteer the brand without being prompted. Here the exact question to be asked can make a big difference; 'What brands of frozen pizza can you think of?' will evoke different brands from the question, 'What brands of frozen food can you think of?' It may be that the most relevant trigger is to suggest a problem or situation rather than a manufacturer's category, e.g. 'What would you do if you had a blocked drain?' or 'What might you drink if you were in a club late on a Friday night?'

Some questionnaires also make a point of registering which brand was mentioned first, or second or third – a concept sometimes known as 'salience', although this word has been used in a number of different ways by different people.

All this is enough to show that 'awareness' is not a simple concept. Assuming a brand name is stored somewhere in the respondent's memory bank, there are many different ways in which we can try to access it. The context in which the brand is brought to mind, or not, may tell us something specific about the nature of the brand relationship. Yet even with awareness, it is doubtful whether one universally relevant measure exists.

It is on the whole true that if a respondent does not even recognise the name of a brand, they are unlikely to have a very meaningful relationship with it. (Even here we need to be alert to special cases, such as the consumer knowing a brand by a name that differs from the manufacturer's terminology.) Prompted awareness, then, could be said to represent a necessary threshold for a brand to pass. Aaker (1995) refers to findings that 'recognition alone can result in more positive feelings towards nearly anything'.

How useful or important it is as a relative measure of the brand's strength is however variable. In many cases prompted awareness will be too high to show much – at 90% or more it is far higher than any penetration figure will be, and variations are probably academic. It is also easy to find high prompted awareness for brands with very low penetration and/or low attractiveness. To quote Aaker again: 'It is one thing to be remembered; it is quite another to be remembered for the right reasons.'

In other categories, however, especially those where there are few rational criteria for decision-making beyond a vague sense of familiarity, being recognised or not recognised may be the key factor in influencing a decision.

Similarly, various types of spontaneous awareness question may be obviously relevant in some instances but less so in others. Where the purchase decision requires spontaneous recall of a brand – needing to ask for a drink at a bar, or telephoning for emergency windscreen replacement – spontaneous awareness is a competitive advantage. However, in situations such as grocery purchase, where brands are displayed side by side, it is less obvious why this should be the case. There is an argument that spontaneous recall is an indicator of preference, but this needs to be argued on a case-by-case basis – and if preference is what we are really measuring here, why not design questions to measure it directly?

Awareness questions appear simple to ask, and superficially make it easy to compare brands in different categories (hence their importance in some proprietary measures, such as the Landor ImagePower study or Equitrend). The various types of awareness measure can indeed tell us a lot about a brand's relationship with the consumer, but they are not so simple nor so universally relevant as they may appear at a superficial glance.

## Associations and beliefs

The network of associations and beliefs that any of us can have about a brand which plays a significant role in our lives can be extremely complex, and the number of questions that can be asked in order to understand how a consumer perceives a brand is virtually without limit. They range from practical measures of factual knowledge or assessment of the brand on functional performance, to highly projective techniques where consumers are asked to describe brands as people or associate them with pictures, smells, or types of music, e.g.

**Scottish Amicable**

*Scottish Amicable is a UK brand selling long-term financial investment products – pensions, endowments, etc. These products are sold through brokers' recommendations but the end-consumer is normally given a choice of suitable brands. Both qualitative and quantitative research showed that in a complex and uncertain area, with no harder criteria for choice, awareness and familiarity was all-important. Consumers assume companies they've heard of are big, established, and secure.*

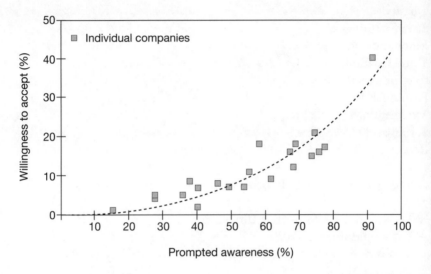

*The advertising strategy therefore concentrated single-mindedly on increasing the brand's prompted awareness and familiarity, and success in doing this led to a parallel increase in sales.*

*Source:* Advertising Works 7 *(Storey, 1993)*

- 'Which of the following credit cards offers free insurance?'
- 'Rank the following brands from 1–7 on "cleaning power".'
- 'If American Express were a person, what would he or she be like?'
- 'What type of music is Heinz?'

A brand can be associated in your mind with:

- Certain types of product

- Types of occasion
- Types of user
- Country of origin
- Colours
- Smells
- Sounds
- Functional benefits

It can be ranked on perceptions of:

- Quality
- Trustworthiness
- Innovation
- Value for money
- Cheap/expensive
- Fashionability
- Modernity
- Sex appeal
- Reliability

It can be described using all forms of analogy or projective task:

- 'Who would it be if it were a film star?'
- 'What would it taste like?'
- 'If Brand B made cars/cakes/clothes, what would they be like?'

It can be described in terms of a two-way relationship (Blackston, 1996):

- 'What does Citibank think of you?'

In other words. the scope is enormous. The only thing that is perhaps surprising is how few of these possibilities are regularly used. In particular the more projective sorts of questions, which have been routinely used in qualitative research for over 30 years, are not often adapted to quantified research, although technically it is not very difficult to do (see Langmaid & Gordon, 1988; Gordon, 1992; Gordon & Restall, 1992).

Likewise the methods that can be used to ask such questions about brands are various, and many of the techniques described elsewhere in this book can be employed. A common method is that of simple ascription ('Which brands fit this description?'); a self-completion questionnaire can acquire a large amount of data very quickly using this approach. Ascription can also be used with visual stimuli, such as photographs, instead of words. More time-consuming, but for some purposes more sensitive, is asking respondents to rate each brand on various types of scale. Different types of analysis, such as correspondence analysis, can be used to summarise and help interpret the data in two- or three-dimensional space, giving rise to brand maps. Other mapping approaches begin by asking respondents to scale brands in terms of their similarity to or difference from each other. We can use open-ended questioning and, of course, all forms of qualitative research.

### Evaluative and descriptive approaches

Another way of subdividing this large area might be to distinguish approaches which are essentially descriptive – Brand A is like this, Brand B is like that – from the more explicitly comparative – Brand A outscores B on this or that dimension. These two notions are not completely distinct (much brand mapping, for example, contains elements of both), but it does describe different approaches to questioning, and also to our interpretation of the data.

If we are in descriptive mode, we are interested in building up a unique picture for each brand in the study. We are alert to very specific associations and meanings that may have no direct equivalent among competitive brands. We will be comparing brand with brand, but so that we can recognise their individual characteristics.

In comparative, or one might say, evaluative mode, we look for dimensions on which we can measure different brands on the same scales. We are focusing on qualities that we expect to be universal to the category, or even to all categories, in order to make evaluative comparisons. To illustrate this point with an analogy: if we were to look in comparative mode at a German shepherd dog and a Dalmatian, we might compare the two breeds' average weight, height, length of hair, lifespan, stamina, etc. In descriptive mode we would begin by observing that the most important difference is that Dalmatians are covered in black spots, and then describe the shape of their head, their history and purpose as a breed, their unique skills and so on.

The purpose of this distinction is not to suggest that one approach is somehow more valuable than the other, but to emphasise their different mindsets. In brand research, we ought to be clear whether we are primarily in one or the other mode, or consciously in both. Otherwise, if a client is expecting an evaluative study, and the researcher is designing a descriptive study, there will be a good deal of frustration on both sides. The two approaches have different uses. From the point of view of understanding the consumer's relationship with the brand, and inspiring future brand strategy and creative work, the descriptive mode is the better one. But when it comes to monitoring trends, or seeking to identify specific areas of weakness or strength, comparative questions are more valuable.

As a general rule good brand management ought to require both. Each can shed an important light on the complex set of meanings and perceptions that the brand represents in the consumer's mind. In addition, each can contribute something to an overall estimate of brand strength. Comparative measures can show where a brand is better on specific qualities. Descriptive measures point out that another part of a brand's strength lies in the unique symbols, values and meanings it has. Comparatively, Coca-Cola might score highly on 'taste', 'refreshment', 'available everywhere', 'for families', etc. – but it would miss out an important element in understanding the brand and its consumer relationship if we did not also know that it was strongly associated with the colours red and white, the classic curved bottle, America, Santa Claus, and polar bears.

### Which attributes matter?

In many types of study, the number of attribute-type questions that can be included in a questionnaire is limited – particularly if scales are being used, or if it is a frequent tracking study. Other types of method, such as self-completion ascription questionnaires, are much less limited as to numbers, although some kind of choice has to be made out of the theoretically unlimited range of possibilities. In any case, the question arises: which attributes or qualities are important for us to know about? Should we include 'a brand for young people' or 'a brand that washes whiter', if we can't have both? And what, if any, is the significance of either attribute?

These are difficult questions, although sooner or later they will occur to anyone involved in this type of research. There are two possible approaches to finding an answer – not mutually exclusive – though it is likely that there will always be an important element of judgement involved. The first approach is preliminary work to elicit relevant and/or discriminating characteristics in the category. This will probably involve qualitative research. It may be relatively unstructured, or make use of more formal elicitation techniques. An alternative or supplementary approach could be to exploit existing knowledge of the consumer by reading earlier reports carefully, or interviewing researchers or others who are expert in the area.

This type of work will produce a wide range of possible ideas, and perhaps some hypotheses as to which are important. The second approach attempts to take things a stage further by quantifying the importance of different attributes within the survey itself. The obvious way of doing this is simply to ask respondents to rank or scale how important to them each attribute is. It has been much doubted, however, whether consumers really understand their own thought processes well enough to give a meaningful answer. If we define an 'important' attribute as one that appears to relate to overall brand attitude or preference (see below) or purchase behaviour, then the idea is arrived at of looking for correlations or patterns in the data. For instance, if attribute A correlates with brand preference more than attribute B, you might conclude that A is the important one. It is sometimes said in this type of analysis that A is a 'driver' of brand choice.

Modern computing power makes this kind of analysis relatively accessible and it may provide some valuable insights. It is nevertheless subject to the same caveat as all attempts to model human decision processes – that is isn't necessarily that simple. There are problems of confusing cause and effect: do I choose Persil because I believe it washes whiter, or do I believe it washes whiter because I use it? Or do people for whom whiteness is important choose Persil for a different reason – one, perhaps, that is far harder to put into words?

## Attitude and loyalty measures

There is, perhaps, a thin line between asking someone to rate a brand on 'quality' and asking them to express a degree of personal preference for it, but this represents a shift from a question about the respondent's *perception* of the brand to one about their *relationship* with the brand. Ultimately, the bottom-line relevance of all the perceptual material described in the preceding section is that it is assumed to relate to consumer behaviour – it influences or explains their buying the brand, staying with the brand, perhaps paying more for the brand. It is possible to observe the results of this behaviour directly in the form of sales (see above), but this alone still begs a question highly relevant to the original issue of brand strength; they may be buying our brand today, but how likely are they to go on buying it tomorrow? Are they simply buying out of habit and inertia, or do they actively value it and feel close to it? How easy would it be for a competitor to take away our sales?

What is being asked for here is a measure of the consumer's overall attraction to the brand. This is also commonly called 'loyalty', though as we shall see this can be defined in different ways. (It is worth thinking about what the word loyalty meant, before it was borrowed by marketing people. A 'loyal' follower of the king was not just one who fought on his side, but one who would resist bribes or threats to betray him or run away. A 'loyal' football supporter goes to every match, home or away. A 'loyal' friend stands by you when others find reasons to desert you.) Or we could describe what we are looking for here as the consumer's 'attitude' to the brand, in the original and proper sense of the word:

> 'Attitudes are enduring systems of positive or negative evaluations, emotional feelings and pro or con action techniques with respect to social objects.'

> (Krech *et al.*, 1962)

Most of the formative work in attitude research, done in the USA from the 1930s to the 1950s, was applied to social issues that were current at the time: racial prejudice, communism, and religion. The goal was to categorise people along a scale that would reflect their loyalty to, or degree of prejudice against, their church, their country, or a social or ethnic group. This was approached in various ways, such as asking respondents to rank themselves on a set of scales, or to ask them which of a list of statements they agreed with. Note that classic measurement of attitude usually involves more than simply asking the respondent a single question.

Attitudinal measures of brand loyalty, consciously or not, operate in this tradition. One measure that is now in use in many markets around the world is Jan Hofmeyr's Conversion Model, which uses a proprietary set of questions to classify all members of a population as follows with regard to a brand (Heath, 1997):

- Buyers:      – Entrenched
                     – Average
                     – Shallow
                     – Convertible
- Non-buyers: – Available
                     – Ambivalent
                     – Weakly unavailable
                     – Strongly unavailable

Interestingly this particular model was originally devised to measure people's attachment to religion (hence its name). It was then used to track degree of loyalty to a political party in South Africa.

Many other forms of question have been devised. Some are very simple – the bipolar scale on which respondents rate each brand between 'For me' and 'Not for me'. Others set up a number of phrases ranging from 'the only brand I would ever use' to 'a brand I would never use in any circumstances'. Some will take the view that the exact wording of such a scale needs to vary from one category to another – what is an appropriate question for a financial product changed once in 40 years will be different from a question about a confectionery brand. Alternatively you could take the view that overall brand attitude is the same as preference, or at least that a preference question (such as a constant sum) will represent it as well as anything.

Either way, these measures of overall attachment, loyalty, or preference appear to represent something very close to our original notion of brand strength, explained as 'underlying consumer demand'. Indeed, up to a point, they do, but any brand attitude measurement invites an important question:

does it predict future behaviour, or does it merely reflect present or past behaviour?

This hinges on what we know about the relationship between attitude and behaviour. The definition of 'attitude' used above includes pro or con action techniques with respect to a social object; in other words, a measure that would predict and perhaps account for behaviour. It is a short step from this to the popular assumption that we first acquire an attitude, and then act on it. Yet even a passing acquaintance with the topic reveals that attitudes are as much a reflection of past or current behaviour as they are predictive of the future – that is, assuming that we have found an attitude measure that relates to behaviour at all.

It is certainly easy to find questions that appear to predict future behaviour but don't, such as asking people what brand they intend to buy next time. If the number intending to buy were higher than the actual brand share, we would probably expect this to mean that brand share was about to go up, but experiments have shown that the reverse is true. People's answers to the question actually lag behind their behaviour – they still believe they are loyal to a brand after they have stopped buying it (Bird & Ehrenberg, 1966, 1967). This is not to say that attitude scales cannot be predictive, but before using one it is worth looking for evidence that it is not merely a rear-view mirror.

Even if an attitude scale is reflecting current behaviour rather than the future, it is at least a good measure of how the brand is perceived now. Another way of measuring current loyalty, if we have panel data, is to examine consumers' actual behaviour. Here, surely, we can see from their actions how many are more loyal and how many less so.

If we look at any consumer panel data at the individual level, we see a complex reality. In any given period, some consumers may have bought into a category many times, some only once or twice, some not at all. Among those who bought in the category, there will be a wide distribution of frequency for buying a particular brand: some will not have bought it at all, some will have bought it once only, while others have bought nothing else, and all points in between (100% brand loyalty is however generally rare, and most 100% loyalists in the behavioural sense are those who bought into the category only once anyway).

Out of the many analyses that can be done with this complex database, the one most commonly proposed as a measure of brand strength is that known as 'Share of Category Requirements', or sometimes the more concise 'Share of Requirements' (hereafter SOR). One way of operationalising this (not the only way) is to look at the proportion of all Brand X buyers for whom the brand represents 50% or higher of their total category purchasing. The assumption here is that those who buy Brand X more than half the time are more 'loyal' to the brand than the rest – and that brands which have more such 'loyal' buyers are stronger. It has also been suggested that these brands are more profitable.

Larry Light (1994) illustrates this argument with an artificial example. Imagine three brands: Brand A is bought by 100% of the population 15% of the time; Brand B is bought by 15% of the population 100% of the time; and Brand C is bought by half of the population 30% of the time. Each, therefore, has an identical 15% market share. It is claimed that Brand B, which has the most 'loyal' user base, is the strongest of the three – and because of this, and because of likely economies in targeting, the most profitable.

Some of this is intuitively appealing. We would expect someone who buys a brand nine times out of ten to be more positively disposed and 'loyal' to that brand than someone who buys it only once out of ten (allowing for external constraints such as distribution). While this may be a reasonable way of distinguishing between individuals, it is questionable whether or not it distinguishes between brands in a market. This is because the hypothetical brand cases put by Light are never found in real markets. Andrew Ehrenberg and his colleagues, by empirical analysis of purchasing patterns, repeated in many categories and markets over a period of nearly 40 years, have shown consistently that the distribution of SOR is highly predictable. If certain facts are established – the brand's share, the number of brands and the frequency of purchase in the category – then buying patterns closely follow a model named after the French mathematician, Dirichlet (Ehrenberg, 1988). So every brand, in fact, has more or less the same spread of loyal and occasional buyers.

It is true, however, that bigger brands predictably have *relatively* more SOR buyers than small brands. This phenomenon has been observed by Garth Hallberg (1995), who has used it to make a case that developing more loyal buyers leads to success, but this reasoning is probably fallacious. There is, at least, a much simpler explanation of the finding – it is a simple mathematical effect discovered by an American sociologist, William McPhee, in 1963, and christened by him 'Double Jeopardy', because smaller brands are doubly disadvantaged – they have fewer buyers, and those buyers buy the brand less often (for the explanation, see Ehrenberg *et al.*, 1990). None of this proves that SOR analysis will *never* show anything useful, but the data have to be interpreted against the *expected* findings (based on the Dirichlet model), not just looked at naively.

## Brand strength and brand size: a summary of the issues

In view of what we said earlier about the relationship between attitudes and behaviour, might we not expect to find that other types of measure also tend to vary more or less predictably with brand size?

**Table 4.1**

|  | Cornflakes (%) | All Bran (%) |
| --- | --- | --- |
| Tastes nice | 64 | 10 |
| Easy to digest | 60 | 19 |
| Popular with all the family | 61 | 5 |
| The kind you come back to | 65 | 4 |
| Reasonably priced | 59 | 5 |
| Average | 62 | 9 |
| Buy regularly | 48 | 7 |

Abridged from Barwise & Ehrenberg (1985)

This is in fact the case. It is a main finding of Ehrenberg's work on buying behaviour that within a category big brands are big because in any given period of analysis they are bought by more people. That is to say, differences in brand size are explained by huge variations in penetration between brands, and very much less affected by the small and mostly predictable variations in average weight of purchase (Ehrenberg & Scriven, 1995).

What follows from this should not really surprise us. In the normal case, the bigger brands will enjoy higher awareness, whether we measure spontaneous, prompted, or top of mind. More respondents will rate the bigger brands on more dimensions – people are much more likely to express opinions on brands they have bought. Thus survey research on brand attributes of bigger brands generally shows lots of figures similar to those in Table 4.1. The fact that Cornflakes scores much higher attributions on everything tells us nothing beyond the fact that many more people are buying it. Certainly if we were to take any of these figures in isolation and conclude, for example, that Cornflakes is considered as better tasting than All Bran, it would be a grave error. What we can do, however, is look at the attributes where All Bran differs from the proportion of Cornflakes figure that we would expect, either by graphing or by calculating a 'different from expected' number. It is these variations from the pattern that are the revealing part of this table. Another way of allowing for this is to examine the beliefs and attitudes among each brand's buyers only.

This is a practical matter of interpretation, reasonably well recognised but still worth repeating. It raises, however, a more difficult question. If all our measures of 'brand strength' are tending to vary with a brand's size, is the whole exercise a pointless pursuit? Is brand strength more or less the same as brand size, whatever we do? Will a big brand always, necessarily, be 'stronger' than a small brand? Is there any way in which All Bran could be stronger than Cornflakes?

---

**Alliance & Leicester**

*In 1985 the Alliance and the Leicester Building Societies merged. From a position of being ninth and tenth largest societies the merged society was sixth largest. It was hoped that this increase in size would result in a greater share of new mortgage and savings business. Unfortunately it did not. In fact, share of business fell, interest rates were cut to attract more money, and profits were squeezed.*

*Analysis showed that share of new savers and new mortgages was closely correlated with a measure of 'propensity to use', which in turn closely related to spontaneous awareness. The Alliance & Leicester was only ninth in terms of both propensity to use and awareness, although it was now sixth in size. High-profile brand advertising over a number of years improved the brand's spontaneous awareness and acceptability and turned the Alliance & Leicester into one of the most successful top ten building societies.*

*Source:* Advertising Works 7 *(Collin, 1993)*

---

Once again, it all depends on what we mean by 'strong'. Within the same category, a bigger brand is almost certainly, on most definitions, bound to be stronger than a small one. It has more buyers, it has more loyal buyers, it has more distribution, it makes more money, it is worth more on a balance sheet. However, there are many possible dimensions to strength, and what is of interest to the brand manager is to know on what dimensions, if any, the brand is weaker (or stronger) than might be expected.

It also depends on what we mean by 'big'. All Bran is a smaller brand than Cornflakes in the cereal category, but it may be brand leader in the high fibre sector. One of the secrets of intelligent brand research lies in correct definition of the brand's competitive set – sometimes, in itself, a question for research. (Where a brand's loyalty patterns differ significantly from the Dirichlet model, this is usually an indication that the brand should be considered in its own sector rather than as part of a larger category; an example might be Sensodyne toothpaste, whose 'strength' as a brand would be better explained as being brand leader in the 'sensitive teeth' sector than as a small brand in all toothpaste.) A brand leader in a small category might be said to be as 'strong' in its own way as a brand leader in a category ten times as large. It has to be said, however, that most forms of brand evaluation will not automatically show this. This is also true of financial valuation of brands, which are discussed below.

# Brand valuation for financial purposes

## *Why brand valuation is done*

There are several reasons for putting a monetary value on a brand: we will explain the three most obvious ones (for others, and the best detailed explanation of the whole subject, see Haigh, 1996).

### *When the brand is bought and sold*

We have seen that brand names are increasingly bought and sold, usually for prices well in excess of any tangible asset value that is associated with them. Sometimes this takes place as part of the take-over or merger of an entire company, such as the take-over of Rowntree by Nestlé. Also, often, companies will divest themselves of brands which no longer form part of their own strategy for the future. In the last ten years, for instance, CPC in the UK alone has bought brands including Ambrosia, Marmite, and Bovril from Beechams, who themselves previously bought these from Cavenham Foods.

### *To include the brand as an intangible asset on a balance sheet*

Paying a lot of money for an intangible asset such as a brand puts a company into an anomalous position under most countries' accounting rules. It has, in effect, paid out a large lump of shareholders' money, but has nothing to show for it – nothing, at any rate, that can be included on a balance sheet, which traditionally has only concerned itself with things that 'can be kicked'. The money paid out therefore has to be written off as a trading loss over a limited period of time, and the company's assets have been, officially, reduced. This can create problems; for instance, if the company wants to borrow money or issue more shares, their scope to do this may be limited by the scale of the assets on the balance sheet.

It was thus for essentially accounting reasons that some inventive businesses, in countries where accounting rules allowed it, began including brands at their take-over value on their balance sheets. Whether this should be allowed or not is still a controversial issue, but it is really a matter for accountants more than for market researchers (see the Afterword to Chapter 3 for an update on this debate).

It is a short step from valuing a brand that has been bought to valuing one that has been created in a similar way. Indeed it can be argued that allowing one kind of brand to be included as an asset and not the other gives rise to its own anomalies and distortions. The practice therefore developed, pioneered by Grand Met in the UK, of valuing all a company's brands as a balance sheet asset.

*For internal planning purposes*

Once the practice of putting a value on brands began to develop, companies who had done it sometimes found that the process was very valuable for planning purposes as well as for financial reasons. The financial value was a yardstick that enabled different brands to be compared and could give insights into their relative strength and potential; moreover, the process of valuation involved an in-depth scrutiny of all the brands on a comparable basis which could add to its usefulness for management. So brand valuation became a valued consultancy tool.

The idea of valuing brands in this way was initially hailed as a great leap forward by the advertising and marketing professions. It was suggested that annual brand valuations should provide performance goals for managers; the general assumption was that when companies started targeting the value of their brands, it would shift the focus away from the short-term pressure to sales and profits, and they would see the wisdom of maintaining marketing and advertising investments. It is very doubtful whether this logic actually follows. Whatever the usefulness of brand valuation, it is unlikely to make much difference to the way managers regard short-term profitability. This is because of the way brand valuation is done, which will now be briefly explained.

## How brand valuation is done

There are various possible approaches to valuing a brand, but we will only concern ourselves here with the one that has become dominant (the others are well-described in Haigh (1996)). The basic principle is simple – the value of a brand, like any other source of income, is based on a forecast of the amount of profit that is expected from it during the foreseeable future (which in financial terms is usually up to about ten years). This is derived by projecting forwards the brand's existing performance, and multiplying this by a factor that takes into account both the estimated opportunity to grow the brand and the downside risk. The most tangible part of this equation is the brand's current performance. The most reliable way for a manager to increase a brand's value, then, may well be to increase its short-term sales or profits – exactly what the marketing people imagined brand valuation might discourage.

A number of different considerations are used in estimating the 'multiplier'. Brand leadership is, sensibly, considered as a plus; everything we know about brands indicates that leaders are a sounder bet than other brands. It includes consideration of legal equities, such as patents, names and symbols, and contracts or agreements that go with the name. Note that while these are 'intangible', they are a different class of asset from everything that we have talked about in this chapter, or that lies in the province of market research. In fact data that relate to the consumer are only one element of several that contribute to this figure.

It will be clear that however well-disciplined and comparable the process, and however diligent and insightful the valuers, a brand's financial value is at bottom a forecast multiplied by an estimate – not an absolute or objective figure. In fact the scope for creating different brand values is even wider than these remarks might imply. One potential buyer of the brand might have reason to believe that their company, with its skills, scale and synergy, could make a great deal more profit out of a brand than the existing owner; in which case the value they would be prepared to pay for the brand could be considerably greater than the brand's value to the existing owner. (Accounting rules do specify that balance sheet valuations must be based on the existing brand ownership, and on its existing products.) This concept will be easily understood by anyone who has played Monopoly, has been cash-rich and needs one last property to complete a set. It explains why brand values in take-overs so often vastly exceed existing estimates; this may indicate more about the weakness of the existing management than the drawbacks of conventional accounting.

None of this is meant as an attack on, or a criticism of brand valuation practices. It is, however, intended to show that financial valuation of a brand, for whatever purpose, is a very different thing from brand evaluation based solely on market research techniques. The latter is a snapshot, at one point in time, intended to reflect what and how much the brand means to its public; the former is an attempt to estimate the monetary worth of the brand to an owner or potential owner. The financial figure is derived from many sources of information besides consumer research.

## A note on 'brand equity'

I have come almost to the end of this chapter, and, as the attentive reader may have noticed, almost without using the expression 'brand equity'. What does this popular phrase signify, and why have I avoided it?

The word 'equity' has been borrowed from finance, and its popularity reflects a general realisation that a brand can be an asset. So far so good. The reason I personally dislike it is that it is used, in practice, to refer to some quite different things. Sometimes the expression is used for what we have mostly called consumer brand strength; sometimes it is used (and it may be in the plural) to refer to descriptive aspects of a brand, its symbols or consumer imagery; and because of its financial origin, it frequently implies, at least, the financial valuation of a brand. This is dangerous, because it suggests to the unwary that all these things are essentially the same, but as I hope has been shown, among other things, in this chapter – they are not. I have also shown that it's possible to review the entire subject without once using the e-word.

## Practical conclusions

I set out to show that there is no single measure of 'brand strength'. There are, however, many different measures possible which each tell something different about the strength or weakness of a brand, and the nature of its relationship with the consumer. True, most of these measures do tend to vary in line with brand size or share, and an analysis of a brand's strength should never ignore its market performance; but this is not invariable, and it is often where the measures vary from what we would otherwise expect that they give the most useful clues.

Quite apart from measuring a brand's performance on linear scales, an important part of the brand's meaning to the consumer is revealed in a more descriptive analysis of the relationship. This should not be overlooked, nor should the availability of more projective techniques and qualitative research.

Despite a popular assumption to the contrary, consumer research does not automatically translate into a financial valuation of a brand. At best it may offer some input into a broader analysis.

What then should the brand manager be looking for? It makes sense to monitor a number of different aspects of brand performance. These should include: an intelligent awareness of trends in the market; relevant measures of awareness; some overall measure of consumer attachment or loyalty; and a more specific appraisal of the brand's distinctive strengths and characteristics in the consumer's mind. David Aaker (1995) suggests that a brand monitoring process should be designed for each brand, giving regard to its individual strategy and marketplace.

There are also available a number of more or less standardised methods of monitoring brands. There are benefits in buying into a standardised methodology; it enables comparisons to be made across categories and markets, and can be interpreted relative to a large database. The trade-off, of course, is that it is further away from Aaker's ideal of a tailor-made approach.

Finally, branding, like language, is a fascinating and important topic which we cannot ignore, but where good theory is still lagging some way behind practice. There is still plenty of room for controversy on many of the issues raised here. I have tried not to be too controversial, but I cannot promise that I have avoided it. There are now some excellent books on brand theory and practice; there is also a lot of woolly thinking and slack terminology, not always helped by clever packaging on the part of research companies and advertising agencies. (I do not mean any criticism here of the products themselves that are packaged in this way.) Those who buy, design or use brand research should be clear about what they are looking for and what they are getting. I hope that this chapter will at least provide a useful map of the overall territory that will help them to do this.

# References

Aaker, D. (1995) *Building Strong Brands*. The Free Press, New York.

Axelrod, J.N. (1992) The use of experimental design in monitoring brand equity. Paper given at ESOMAR seminar 'The Challenge of Branding Today and in the Future?', Brussels, October, pp. 13–26.

Barwise, P. & Ehrenberg, A.S.C. (1985) Consumer beliefs and brand usage. *Journal of the Market Research Society* 27(2), pp. 81–93.

Bird, M. & Ehrenberg, A.S.C. (1966, 1967) Intentions to buy and claimed brand usage. *Operational Research Quarterly* 17, pp. 27–46 and 18, pp. 65–66.

Blackston, M. (1996) Corporations are people too. In *Researching Brands* (Caller, L., ed.). New Monograph Series vol. 3. ESOMAR, Amsterdam.

Broadbent, S. (1990) Modelling beyond the blip. *Journal of the Market Research Society* 32(1), pp. 61–102.

Broadbent, S. (1992) Using data better – a new approach to sales analyses. *Admap*, January, pp. 48–54.

Collin, W. (1993) Alliance & Leicester building society – advertising effectiveness 1987–1991. In *Advertising Works 7* (Baker, C., ed.), pp. 359–382. NTC Publications, Henley-on-Thames.

Cooper, C., Cook, L. & Jones, N. (1991) How the chimps have kept PG Tips brand leader through 35 years of intense competition. In *Advertising Works 6* (Feldwick, P., ed.), pp. 3–25. NTC Publications, Henley-on-Thames.

Crimmins, J.C. (1992) Better measurement and management of brand value. *Journal of Advertising Research* 32(4), pp. 11–19.

Ehrenberg, A.S.C. (1988) *Repeat Buying*. Revised edition. Charles Griffin & Company, London; OUP, New York.

Ehrenberg, A.S.C., Goodhardt, G.J. & Barwise, T.P. (1990) Double jeopardy revisited. *Journal of Marketing* 54, July, pp. 82–91.

Ehrenberg, A.S.C. & Scriven, J. (1995) Added values or propensities to buy. JOAB Report 1, South Bank Business School, London.

Gordon, W. (1992) Researching a brand. In *Understanding Brands* (Cowley, D., ed.). Kogan Page, London.

Gordon, W. & Restall, C. (1992) Brands – the missing link: understanding the emotional relationship. Paper given at ESOMAR seminar 'The Challenge of Branding Today and in the Future?', Brussels, October, pp. 145–162.

Haigh, D. (1996) *Brand Valuation*. Institute of Practitioners in Advertising, London.

Hallberg, G. (1995) *All Consumers Are Not Created Equal*. John Wiley & Sons, New York.

Heath, R. (1997) Brand commitment as a predictor of advertising effect. *Admap*, April, pp. 53–57.

Krech, D., Crutchfield, R.A. & Ballachey, E.L. (1962) *Individual in Society: A Textbook of Social Psychology*. McGraw Hill, New York.

Langmaid, R. & Gordon, W. (1988) A great ad, pity they can't remember the brand – true or false? Paper given at the Market Research Society conference, Brighton, March.

Light, L. (1994) *The Fourth Wave: Brand Loyalty Marketing*. Coalition for Brand Equity, New York.

Ries, A. & Trout, J. (1993) *The 22 Immutable Laws of Marketing*. Harper Collins, London.

Storey, R. (1993) Scottish Amicable – how it paid to be amicable. In *Advertising Works 7* (Baker, C., ed.), pp. 333–358. NTC Publications, Henley-on-Thames.

# Part Two

# On Advertising

Chapter 5

# Why Don't Ad Agencies Get on Better with Ad Researchers?

## Introduction

In the first chapter of *The Advertising Budget*, Simon Broadbent made an important disclaimer:

> 'For the most part I write of a single marketer who makes rational and honest decisions. The complications of company politics and company marketing strategy are outside the scope of this book.'

> (Broadbent, 1989, p. 13)

This is a useful assumption to make, perhaps a necessary one – advertising planning is demanding enough in a purely intellectual sense without the 'complications of company politics', but in the real world these are not so easy to put to one side. In this chapter the emphasis will be on the importance of the 'people factor' in advertising research.

Imagine a basic triangle, whose three points are the advertiser (what we in ad agencies call 'the client'), the advertising agency, and the research agency. This is an oversimplification, since each of these organisations inevitably has its own internal divisions and conflicts – between marketing and finance, between brand groups and senior management, between account groups and creatives, and, I suppose, between research executives and statisticians

---

Originally published as 'Agency, client and researcher: the eternal triangle?' *Admap*, June 1997.

and field managers, and so on. These do impact quite often on our triangle, but in order to build an argument I'll choose to oversimplify the picture.

There are many ways in which these three parties interact, but for now let's imagine the context is some kind of advertising evaluation research – say, an advertising pretest, or something like a tracking study debrief. This is where conflicts in the relationship are most likely to occur, and this is the sort of situation that most people have in mind when they talk about 'the relationship between planners and researchers'. No doubt many readers will have at least one example from their own experience, where this situation has been a highly stressful one for some, if not all, of those concerned.

When we're in such a situation, the natural human tendency is to blame the conflict on the malevolence or stupidity of the other lot. 'Those researchers don't know a thing about advertising', 'They're out to get us', 'That arrogant ad agency lot didn't listen to a word and just tried to rubbish the research'. People *are* malevolent or stupid from time to time, but I believe the majority of these conflicts are not caused by simple ill-will or ignorance on the part of the individuals concerned. In fact, I think it's generally true that if you took the same individuals and put them into different roles, most of the same conflicts would still occur. In other words, the conflicts are inherent in the *system* – so if we want to minimise unproductive conflicts, we first need to understand how the system works.

What then are the underlying factors that so often lead to conflict in the system which this triangle represents? Let's consider an imaginary situation. It's not intended to be typical, just one possible example. We're at a tracking study debrief, a few months into the new advertising campaign. At the table (among others) are the marketing manager of Plumtrees Jam, and the account director from well-known ad agency, Whinge Cavil and Grouse. The debrief is being given by the senior research executive from A Big Research Agency, or ABRA as it's usually known.

The marketing manager has bought into the new, slightly controversial campaign after a great deal of argument with the agency, and several rounds of qualitative pretesting. He's personally comfortable with the campaign now, but under strong pressure from his colleagues and his bosses to show that it's working – and that it's not offending people or trivialising the product, as some influential people fear it might. He will be personally embarrassed if the campaign fails, but believes he could survive having to ditch the campaign as long as he were to cut his losses and do it early enough.

The agency account director does not fully appreciate the pressure the marketing manager is under. He assumes that now the campaign has been sold, he will defend it all the way. He personally loves the campaign, not just because it is already up for a creative award, has been 'choice of the week' in

*Campaign* and has enhanced his reputation in the agency, but because he genuinely believes in it – he has been to plenty of group discussions where he has seen people clearly enjoying it, and talking about it with enthusiasm. If this research says anything against the campaign, he'll find it very hard to believe.

The research executive has handled this account for about four years, and tracked the two previous campaigns. She's very proud of what ABRA does and believes her company is at the forefront of understanding tracking research. She also values her own and her company's integrity, and makes a real effort not to be influenced by what she thinks the client or the agency might want to hear. She'll be even-handed in presenting the data and won't draw firm conclusions where the data do not justify them. She also knows, however, that the new marketing manager, who inherited ABRA from his predecessor, thinks ABRA is expensive, and isn't convinced its results are sufficiently useful. In fact he still rather favours a rival tracking outfit he used to work with at his previous company. So she's also under pressure to produce some clear, actionable results.

All of these people are honest, committed and genuinely want to do their best. (Let's assume they're all nice people, too.) Nevertheless, they each have a different set of goals and priorities:

- The client's objective is to weigh up the data as an early warning system, especially on certain sensitive measures, and decide whether to ditch the campaign or not.
- The account director believes it is in the client's interest as well as his own to defend the campaign at all costs.
- The researcher wants to be fair and scientific but also to provide as much actionable and useful guidance as she can.

The stage is already set for some kind of conflict. Let's take one possible example. Buried in the data is a figure that says *35% of the people who recall the campaign dislike something about it*. The marketing manager knows this will be like a red rag to a bull if the managing director ever sees it. The account director believes this is irrelevant, as all strong campaigns tend to polarise opinions and lots of other measures are very positive. The research executive won't arbitrate in this dispute, but just points out that 35% is considerably above their average for this question.

Whichever way the decision goes, the agency leaves the meeting cursing the researchers who (nearly) killed the campaign, the researcher leaves the meeting complaining that the agency, as expected, was totally defensive, and the client may leave confirmed in his belief that the research wasn't at all helpful.

This, as I say, is one of the many stories in the naked city of advertising research. Many aspects could have been different. The marketing manager might have been the one who was desperate to defend the campaign because he couldn't afford to change it, or he might already have been committed to killing it. The ad agency, believe it or not, is not always defensive – they might be keen to move on to what they think is a better campaign; but this story will do to illustrate some general points. Let's try and extract what these might be.

## Each player has different goals and priorities

At one level all three points of the triangle ought to share a common goal – 'to produce the most effective advertising'. This would indeed be a positive point to start from, and we shall return to it later, but 'politics is the art of the possible'. It would be nice to see market research as an unencumbered search for truth. In reality, it is one ingredient in a number of different agendas. People are concerned about their own jobs, about keeping their clients, about maintaining their credibility, about looking good, about pleasing their colleagues; not just because all these things make them feel more comfortable (though that in itself can be a powerful motive), but also because they may judge these things are necessary to their achieving other goals, which they may see as more important.

## Each comes from a different company culture

The marketing manager works for a multinational corporation where the main corporate goal is delivering the bottom line and failure is not tolerated. Sober suits and ties have recently been replaced by the new uniform of chinos and polo shirts, but as he is not a board director he still has to get his own coffee from the machine. Communication is by memo and meetings are formal and sometimes dangerous.

The account director works in an agency where the main corporate goal is producing famous advertising and the worst sin is losing favour with the creative department. When not meeting clients he wears jeans to work. Communication largely takes place in the corridor or the pub, or when walking into other people's offices.

The research executive works in a large, open plan, out-of-town site, which aspires to the atmosphere of a university campus, and the one thing you're not allowed to be is ignorant. She dresses to match her clients but many of the office back-up staff have pony tails or earrings. Communication takes place largely by e-mail and mobile phone.

While not the most important area of difference, these backgrounds may lead to each player having different norms and expectations about the sort of meeting they would like the debrief to be. The client is prepared for a relatively formal political game; the ad person would like it to be a friendly and personal chat; the researcher is planning for a dispassionate examination of evidence.

## Each has a different mental model of how advertising works

'Mental models' are our assumptions, generally unconscious and therefore uncriticised, about how things work. Since no one quite knows how advertising really does work – it's too complicated – our dominant mental models become of great importance. Typically, the three companies here have three different models:

(1) In the client's organisation no one has ever explicitly formulated a theory of how advertising works, so like Keynes' 'practical men' they have a set of assumptions which they take to be 'common sense': that advertising is about selling to new customers, that you should give as many facts as you can about the product, that headlines and pictures shouldn't be humorous or eccentric. They do not realise that their 'common sense' is really a folk memory of a theory created by an American copywriter (Claude Hopkins) over 70 years ago, based on his experience of selling tractors and trusses by mail order to mid-Western prairie farmers.

(2) In the ad agency their mental model of advertising is quite different, but not necessarily much more sophisticated. They like humour, they like intriguing headlines and odd pictures, they don't believe in long copy; and like the client company, they don't know that their version of 'common sense' is based on a research method invented over 70 years ago by a young mid-Western psychology professor (Daniel Starch), who encouraged advertisers to judge an advertisement's success by the number of people who remembered seeing it in a magazine.

(3) The research company of course has a much more complex and scientific model of how advertising works, which conveniently depends on a number of measures that have been included for years in their tracking studies.

This is a slight caricature, perhaps. However, an issue such as the one we invented – 35% of respondents 'disliked' something about the ads – can be interpreted in quite different ways, not just because people are prejudiced for or against the campaign, but because they start from entirely different assumptions about whether people need to like an ad, how many of them need to like it, and how much. The agency man's mental model rates a strong reaction as desirable, even if some of it is negative. The client company's mental model rates anyone disliking the ads as a problem. The researcher's mental model must attribute some significance to this figure, because otherwise why did they ask the question? Yet in the absence of 'scientific' evidence, she may be ambivalent about what this is.

## Each has a different concept of what constitutes valid 'evidence'

The marketing manager, in our story, is mostly concerned with what John May (1981) once called 'organisational validity'. Within his corporate culture, numbers have high 'organisational validity', and the way his superiors will react to the data is more important to him than what the data 'really' mean.

The researcher here has a more scientific concept of validity. She believes her figures are meaningful because she knows how the sample was constructed and because of experimental work her company may have done to relate such data to other things, e.g. sales. She won't pretend it's perfect, but by the standards of scientific research she thinks it's pretty good and as objective as she can make it.

However, our advertising account director is much more convinced by the evidence of his own eyes and ears. He's been in group discussions where he's actually *seen* people laughing at the ads and saying how good they are; he's had similar reactions from his friends, his colleagues, and other people whose judgement he respects. Numbers on a chart, though they have huge weight for his client, do little to change his beliefs.

## Three's a crowd?

So much for the differences which partially explain the conflicts that occur. What about the dynamics of the relationship – how does each party see the others?

A triangle can be seen as an inherently unstable pattern, as in the 'eternal triangle' where two people fight for the affection of a third. Perhaps there's an element of this in our triangle: the ad agency and the research agency can see themselves as vying for influence, or even, in a kind of subconscious sibling rivalry, for the affections of their mutual client. The other unstable pattern in a threesome is that two members of the group form an alliance, formally or otherwise, in order to control or put pressure on the third. In this situation, the commonest alliance is where the client uses the research agency as an ally to help control the advertising agency. This is easily rationalised as maintaining the researcher's integrity and independence, but the idea of using the research company to 'police' the advertising is not the most constructive way to proceed. If the ad agency really needs policing, perhaps the client should look for a more trustworthy agency with whom they can have a more open relationship. It is the ad agency which ultimately has to make use of the research company's findings, and if these are imposed by force rather than by agreement, the results are unlikely to be happy ones. This approach can even lead to clients deliberately instructing researchers to keep apart from the advertising agency, for fear of being influenced or compromised by too much fraternisation – and perhaps, fear of an unholy alliance between the two agencies to exploit the client?

I believe all such alliances create more problems than they solve, and I would like to suggest a different image for the triangle – not as an unbalanced relationship, but as the three legs of a tripod, the minimum number which are needed to achieve stability. Bearing this image in mind, how could we improve the working relationships between ad agencies and researchers, especially in those areas which are most prone to conflict?

First of all, we should not expect to avoid differences of opinion and different points of view, sometimes quite heated ones. One reason why people argue so intensely about advertising is that they care passionately about it. Clients care about how they spend their hard-earned money; agencies care about doing good work; researchers care about helping them do these things. We could start by recognising this fact: we argue, because we are all passionate about what we do.

## Conclusions

Perhaps we could stop these differences becoming too acrimonious or counterproductive, by building on some of the observations I've already offered.

Agency, researchers and advertisers could begin by focusing on their common objectives, and by reconciling their mental models. To say, 'we all want to make the advertising more effective', does not in itself go far enough; it begs the question of what *effective* means. This includes a number of strategic dimensions which often cause grounds for misunderstanding later:

the overall objective (in sales or business terms) for the advertising; the target audience (which the research should reflect); and some shared model, however difficult it may be to express, of how the advertising is intended to influence them. I do not mean, here, the artificial imposition of 'action standards', often with no rational basis other than that they appear to be 'measurable'; I *do* mean full briefings of the researchers by agency and client together before the research begins, to negotiate a common understanding of what everyone expects to happen.

All concerned could try to achieve a better understanding of each other's point of view. There are too few people (and I'm not one myself) who have working experience in both research and advertising agencies, and/or on the client side. The opportunity to get to know each other outside the potentially confrontational situation of that debrief should be taken, and exchange visits spending a few days in each others' organisations are even better. Such contacts can help to break down entrenched prejudices ('all researchers are boring and destructive', 'all advertising people are irresponsible prima donnas') and encourage each party to understand that a broader point of view is possible. Agencies might admit more often that their ads could be improved or changed; researchers could also admit that their data, however good, are never completely unambiguous nor the only kind of evidence on which advertising decisions should be made.

The advertiser can do a great deal to improve the process too. The strategy of 'divide and rule', or using the researcher as external police force, is not compatible with an open and constructive relationship. The client pays the piper and has the power to encourage a three-way relationship, where everyone is made to feel part of the same team working to a common goal.

The client – or at least, the client organisation – also dictates the way everybody is allowed to feel about the prospect of failure. If an agency is made to understand that any adverse judgement of the advertising is *ipso facto* an adverse judgement of the agency, which may well lose them the business, it gives them little option but to defend their work at all costs.

Evaluating advertising and evaluating agency performance should be kept as two separate processes – a good agency may show its quality most clearly in the way it responds to disappointing results, but it can only do this if it's allowed to! Some popular self-help guru has said that there is no such thing as failure, there are only results – from which you have the opportunity to learn. Failure is not the same thing as incompetence. Keith Reinhard, Chairman of DDB, expressed this distinction in a DDB internal publication entitled *The Four Freedoms*: 'It is the job of management to first point talented people in the right direction and then to judge their work. *But if the approach to that work is responsible and intelligent* [my italics], people must never be criticised for daring to fail'. If this were more widely understood in advertising research circles, it would transform the atmosphere in which many a debrief is received.

## References

Broadbent, S. (1989) *The Advertising Budget*. NTC Publications, Henley-on-Thames.

May, J. (1981) Marketing research: illuminating neglected areas. *Journal of the Market Research Society* 23(3), pp. 127–136.

# Chapter 6

# Is There a 'Right Way' to Pre-test Advertising?

## Introduction

'Copy testing' embraces a number of quite radically different techniques, based on different theories and assumptions about how advertising works, and is also a highly competitive marketplace, where the suppliers of each technique tend to stress the merits of their own particular method with a bewildering degree of conviction. The advertiser might well say to himself: 'Surely they can't all be right?', and his advertising agency may well advise him: 'No, none of them is'. We shall try to pick our way through this confusing landscape and review the evidence as fairly as we can.

Before distinguishing the main theories and techniques, let's consider a spectrum of attitudes with which different people approach copy testing research.

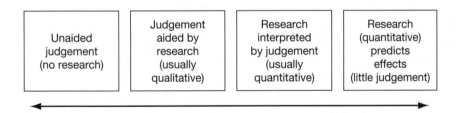

| Unaided judgement (no research) | Judgement aided by research (usually qualitative) | Research interpreted by judgement (usually quantitative) | Research (quantitative) predicts effects (little judgement) |

At the left-hand side of this diagram is a belief that advertising works in ways that are too complex and subtle to be analysed and measured by any

From 'A brief guided tour through the copy-testing jungle', Admap Conference paper, January 1998.

type of research. This attitude will be most obviously found among creative directors, but is also prevalent among other agency staff and even certain clients. For these people, advertising decisions are a matter for pure judgement. One can have some sympathy for this point of view, perhaps more so after spending a long time studying in depth the psychological complexity of the task and the conflicting evidence for any success. It is true that many famous and successful campaigns, including the majority of the IPA Effectiveness Awards winners, have been approved on just this basis.

At the other extreme are the copy testing companies who sell their systems on the promise that they will predict, with a high degree of accuracy, marketplace performance. The prediction will be mainly based on numerical scores which leave little room for personal judgement. Such a claim is understandably attractive to many companies. Not only does it offer to reduce risk and improve efficiency, it means that advertising decisions need no longer be delegated to fallible individual managers. Others, of course, are sceptical.

Between these extremes are two other common positions. Moving across from the left extreme one comes to the belief that judgement is paramount, but can be improved by getting some form of feedback on the advertising from the target group. This need not claim to be very scientific, but represents a more or less informal 'reality check' – is it relevant to them? Do they understand it? Does it seem to interest or involve or amuse them in some way? This is one use of purely qualitative research, and it is a common way of working in most markets around the world. Its proponents argue that what it may lack in scientific rigour, it makes up for in sensitivity, flexibility, and the sense it gives of a direct dialogue with the consumer. Again it is undeniable that many famous, and successful, campaigns have been produced in this way.

This position is closely identified with the British account planning tradition, which was in part a reaction against the more mechanistic forms of advertising research popular in the 1960s. Wherever one is positioned on this spectrum, we should not forget the arguments of writers like Hedges (1974) and King (1967) that there is a great deal more to advertising research than merely evaluation. Without proper strategic and developmental work, evaluative techniques on their own will not be likely to increase the chances of success. This may sound obvious, but in practice the fascination of evaluative research often proves so strong that it uses up a disproportionate share of the research budget. In my experience money can always be found for another round of copy testing, when you wouldn't have a hope of getting it for 'exploratory' research – even though the exploratory research might be more valuable.

One advertiser in the USA spent its entire annual research budget of $300,000 on one proprietary form of persuasion testing. Whatever the merits of this particular technique – and in this case I did not rate them very highly – this meant that their understanding of the consumer was effectively nil, and also meant that producing ads for research was very much a matter of guesswork. Evaluative research, even if well done, is not the answer to all the advertiser's problems. It may be that if budgets are restricted there is more benefit to be had from proper strategic research than from doing any evaluation work at all.

Moving further to the right one finds research which uses predominantly quantitative (but also often qualitative) techniques not to predict sales efficiency directly, but to measure concepts similar to those investigated in qualitative research – impact, comprehension, message recall, liking and so on. The measures are much 'harder' than in qualitative research, but there is still usually a lot of room for judgement and debate about what they actually mean. Will an ad that communicates clearly but is disliked, for instance, perform better than one that is heartily enjoyed but puts a less clear message across?

Moreover, there are intermediate points on such a spectrum. Some users of qualitative research may be strongly ruled by it, others inclined to ignore it if it runs counter to their judgement. Some quantitative systems are more rigorous and predictive than others. Where you wish to position yourself, if you are an advertiser, along this spectrum, will depend partly on what you are prepared to believe about the conflicting claims of the copy researchers. It will also depend on your corporate style and culture. A seat-of-the-pants entrepreneur may feel happiest towards the left; a large, bureaucratically run multinational may prefer to be at the right. If the advertiser and the agency are firmly entrenched at different points on the spectrum, there will be some pain.

Still, wherever you are along this spectrum, you still need to face up to exactly the same questions. What are the clues that will indicate the future success of the ad? Any answers to this question will be based on conscious or unconscious assumptions about the advertising process. Is it important for a successful ad to be remembered, to be liked, to communicate a message which can be verbalised? Does advertising have an immediately measurable effect on propensity to buy, or does this only happen later as a result of repetition or a purchase decision? These are still questions to which there are few answers.

The numbers of different pre-testing systems are legion. DDB produced a directory of those available in the USA alone, which is the size of a telephone book. Fortunately for the sake of a brief paper, the methods do tend to fall into family groups, like the animal kingdom, and I will now attempt the outline of a Linnaean classification. Perhaps the two most useful concepts to help us understand the structure of the copy testing market are 'attitude shift/persuasion' and 'recall/impact and communication'. Both have a long history – attitude shift dates back to Horace Schwerin's theatre tests in the 1950s, while recall can trace its ancestry ultimately to press testing techniques pioneered by Daniel Starch and George Gallup in the 1920s and 1930s.

## Attitude shift or persuasion tests

'Attitude shift' is based on the premise that a change in attitude or propensity to buy the brand takes place around the time of viewing the ad which is predictive of subsequent marketplace behaviour. This attitude shift can be isolated and measured in different ways. The most common is the pre–post test, as devised by Schwerin, and which forms the basis for the ARS system currently operated by research services corporation (rsc) and the Ad*Vantage system of McCollum Spielmann Worldwide (currently licensed in Germany by GfK).

The basic Schwerin-type method may be described as follows. A sample of respondents is invited to a central location to view a television programme, which they are led to believe is the main object of the research. Before the show they are offered participation in a prize draw for a basket of groceries and other products (it could include, for instance, a test drive of a car.) For each item in the basket each respondent selects a favoured brand from a number of alternatives. After the show, which has contained commercial breaks in which the test commercials are seen once or twice by the audience, the prize draw is repeated. Any increase in the percentage of respondents selecting the advertised brand is used as the basis for a persuasion score, which is the main output of the research. There are numerous variations possible on this technique.

Despite its popularity and indeed its ingenuity the pre–post theatre test using a gift choice has been subject to criticism for various kinds of bias and conditioning which may come into it (Twyman, 1973). The alternative design for testing for attitude shift is to use two matched samples, one of which sees the ad, the other only a pack shot. Apart from being a 'purer' design less obviously subject to obscure forms of conditioning, this makes it possible to ask more subtle questions to measure the attitude shift. Instead of the simple two-way choice 'yes/no' in the gift basket, you can rate propensity to buy on a seven-point scale (which Twyman found to correlate with actual behaviour), you can ask other types of image question, and in particular you can identify shifts in intention or favourability among existing brand loyalists, who by definition have nowhere to go to in the gift choice, yet must be recognised as the most important part of the market for any established brand.

A far more basic objection to the whole notion of attitude shift research however is made by those who deny its fundamental assumptions, i.e. (1) that a measurable change takes place at the time of exposure, and (2) that this is a necessary and adequate predictor of subsequent behaviour. This argument has been developed in recent years by Gordon Brown and his colleagues at Millward Brown (Brown, 1991).

Brown's model of how advertising works is very different. He argues that images and associations go into the memory at the time of seeing advertising, but that changes in attitude to the brand are likely to take place later, at the time of purchase or even as a consequence of using the product. Consumers may register a message, but are unlikely to be fully convinced by it, or even to consider it as very relevant to them, until such time as they become actively involved with the product. (The theory has something in common with Krugman (1977), though Brown would disagree with him perhaps on some other points.)

It follows from this that attitude shift measured at the time of exposure will not be a sound predictor of advertising effect. There could be successful ads which would show no immediate attitude shift; moreover, attitude shift which did take place might not reflect all the ways in which advertising works over the longer term to reinforce and condition perceptions of a brand.

Brown believes that certain types of advertising will get predictably good scores in attitude shift research (Farr, 1993). These are what he describes as ads containing 'new news', i.e. new and mainly factual information about the product which prompts an immediate revaluation and curiosity to try. This greatly favours ads for new or relaunched products, and this in turn accounts for the correlation between persuasion scores and short-term sales growth which is shown by the leading practitioners of attitude shift as validation (new products have nowhere to go but upwards!). For established products therefore attitude shift is of little use. Needless to say, its proponents dispute this view (Rosenberg & Blair, 1994).

In a recent experiment (Farr & Brown, 1994) Brown showed that four test commercials registered no positive attitude shift at the time of viewing (using a monadic design with an intention-to-buy question rather than a gift basket), but had a clearly measurable effect on consumer perceptions of the brand when it was actually used.

If you accept Brown's model of advertising, then it is the ability of the advert to put the right images and associations into long-term memory and to link them with the brand that becomes the major predictor of success. Millward Brown's methodology known as the Link Test is in fact an evolution from the other main tradition of copy research, which may be collectively described as *impact and communication,* or *recall.* The typical impact and communication methodologies are described below.

## Impact and communication tests

Rather than attempt to measure a single proxy for behaviour – which is assumed to be unrealistic – the 'impact and communication' test measures a number of intermediate constructs which ultimately trace their ancestry back to such early formulations as Starch's (1923) theory of advertising: to be successful an ad must be *seen – read – believed – remembered – acted upon.* It will typically measure most or all of the following:

- Impact or cut-through
- Recall of brand
- Recall of message and content, to check comprehension and communication
- Likes and dislikes
- So-called 'diagnostic' questions rating attitudes to the ad, e.g. hard to believe, realistic, amusing, boring, etc.

These questions can add up to quite a lengthy interview in which the advert may be exposed two or more times. Characteristically there are quite a lot of open-ended questions as well.

All this produces a great deal of information which can be of great usefulness in understanding how respondents perceive and react to the ad. However, there are in practice some quite complex issues raised:

- How the questions themselves are worded
- How the responses are coded and interpreted

and more fundamentally,

- Which of these constructs or combination of constructs predicts behaviour?
- What level on each scale represents a desirable target?
- What balance of 'good' or 'bad' scores is regarded as satisfactory?

It is for this reason that most impact and communication tests might best be regarded as *aids to judgement* rather than *predictive systems.* What this means, however, is that the data themselves leave a lot of scope for interpretation – and often, in practice – conflict.

While the Starch model looks at first glance like simple common sense, turning it into an operational model raises all sorts of questions about the real importance of each measure. For example:

- Many such tests began by showing the test ad in a reel of other ads ('clutter') to test for *impact* or *cut-through* or *standout*. All these words sound like something that would be desirable in an ad. The assumption seems to be that the more impact an ad has, the more it will be remembered, but after doing such tests for years, Millward Brown discovered that there was very little correlation between scores obtained in a clutter reel and subsequent marketplace recall as measured on a tracking study (Brown, 1991).

- Another very common procedure is to ask respondents what they liked and what they disliked in the ad, and/or to rate their overall 'liking' of the ad on a five-point scale. This can produce some interesting findings, but a huge interpretative leap is required to decide what balance of 'likes' vs. 'dislikes' is desirable or acceptable – if such a question makes sense at all. Is an ad with 10% likes and 5% dislikes better or worse than one with 40% likes and 20% dislikes? Does it matter if 20% of the sample 'dislike' the ad? If not, at what point is it a problem? Interpretation of such answers is often based on very little knowledge, but a great deal of emotion. For some advertisers, the idea that anyone might dislike their advertising is uncomfortable, even though many successful campaigns polarise reactions, and there are well-attested examples of campaigns highly successful in sales terms which very few people 'liked' at all (e.g. Strepsils: White, 1995).

- Another often controversial topic is that of message recall. It requires great care in questioning and interpretation to ensure that ads with a simple, verbalisable message (e.g. 'Cleans clothes with nitric acid') don't automatically perform better than non-verbal ads which may create powerful imagery or emotional reactions that are hard to put into words.

This type of research, if well done by an experienced and sensitive advertising researcher, can be rich and helpful, but it can also turn into a depressing and frustrating experience for the advertising agency as sloppy questions, poor coding, and *non sequiturs* of interpretation based on invalid models of advertising, misrepresent the reality of consumer reaction.

Given the difficulties in making sense of complex and confusing consumer reactions, it can even be tempting to reconsider one of the arguments for attitude shift research, namely that the consumer's memory and interpretation and verbalisation of the ad are merely confusing, and that the psychology of *how* the ad works is, for testing purposes, best left in a black box – attitude shift will go straight to the end result, the increased tendency to buy. To which in turn one might point out that if attitude shift cannot enter the black box, its ability to diagnose what is wrong or right with the advertising, and so to improve it, is going to be extremely limited. And this is indeed a common criticism levelled at attitude shift research – that it offers little diagnostic help.

We therefore would expect to find persuasion tests positioned further to the right on our original spectrum than impact and communication tests.

## Other variations

*Attitude shift* and *recall* define the two main pillars of copy testing. Around them are numerous variations. There are both on-air and off-air testing methods. 'Day after recall' would claim to improve on a hall test of impact and communication by inserting the test ad in a real TV break in a natural viewing situation, and then leaving a time lapse of 24 hours before phoning respondents to ask what they remember from the advertising. (Memory, of course, decays considerably over this period, making 'day after recall', its adherents claim, a more discriminating test of memorability.) The same methodology has been adapted to a form of attitude shift testing (by the American research company ASI).

There are other ingredients which can be added to the basic recipe, a common one of long standing being some mechanical method of registering interest in the ad on a second-by-second basis. (Measurements of eye movement and galvanic skin response have rather fallen out of fashion, though I recently came across a new methodology which involved measuring cerebral activity through electrodes attached to the respondent's head.) There are methodologies which fall between qualitative and quantitative approaches, combining self-completion questionnaires, interest levers, and group discussions.

There are hybrids which combine elements of recall and persuasion, like the 'Sherman Buy Test'. Actually most copy tests include some element of both, but usually it is clear that one aspect is much more important than the other, and there is always the possibility that someone will invent a new one tomorrow. On the whole, however, those commonly used tend to be variations on techniques established many years ago.

But how to choose between them?

## The question of validation

You might think that by this time enough evidence would have been built up to validate one approach over another. Unfortunately the evidence is complex and conflicting, partly because much of the validation work has been produced under the auspices of the research companies themselves, who each naturally tend to stress the merits of their own product. Impressive internal validations will be found in the promotional literature of both the leading persuasion and recall practitioners. Such validations are no doubt based on genuine data; but, inevitably, any research business has an interest in presenting the data to its best advantage. As early as 1965 Fothergill and Ehrenberg (1965) felt obliged to take issue with the validation evidence published by Horace Schwerin, claiming in a highly statistical paper that the way in which the correlation of persuasion scores and sales results had been calculated was such that random numbers would have given the same positive result.

Such genuinely disinterested studies as have been published are unfortunately of little help. In a major study of their single-source test market data (Lodish, 1991), IRI (Information Resources Incorporated) concluded that:

> 'It is very unlikely that there is a strong relationship between standard measures of TV commercial recall and persuasion for established brands and the sales impact of the copy.'

At about the same time the ARF reported on a complex and expensive study (Haley & Baldinger, 1991) which was nevertheless only based on five pairs of commercials. This study suggested that the most successful single measure of predicting sales performance (although it was far from perfect) was a scale of 'liking' – an idea that caused some consternation in traditional US advertising research circles. However, its overall diplomatic conclusions were that 'copy testing works!' and 'no methods can be rejected based on this research'. (The ARF is principally funded by research companies.) Others, including myself, have looked at the same ARF data and drawn somewhat different conclusions (Feldwick, 1992; Rossiter & Eagleson, 1994). Like many a copy test itself, the ARF's study has given everyone more data to argue about.

It is unlikely that there is one answer to all circumstances. It is now widely recognised that different ads work in differing ways, and therefore the answer may be 'horses for courses'. Such a strategy has support from no less than George Gallup:

'Every school [of copy testing] claims to be the school. But I think that the most useful, truthful way of thinking of copy testing is to regard all of the methods as useful and serving a given purpose. There isn't any method that will cover the waterfront. This is the mistake all schools of thought make. They believe that if they find a cure for a headache, it will cure flat feet; but one must know the limitations of each method.'

(Bartos, 1986)

Although I have my own preferences and prejudices, and although I've seen plenty of evidence – unfortunately, unpublishable – that none of the principal methodologies is infallible, I'm not going to end this chapter by telling anyone what they should do. I don't intend to adjudicate in the long-running battle between persuasion and recall, qualitative and quantitative, on-air or off-air, and all the rest of it.

However, I will point out that in copy testing you have a number of choices. If you regard copy testing as potentially important to your business, you should take these choices seriously, and not just give the business to the first plausible research company you meet. What they offer is, as I hope I've shown, very different, and often mutually incompatible.

The first choice is where you see yourself on the spectrum. Do you believe in the power of well-informed judgement, or are you prepared to back a system? Are you happier with the immediate human contact in qualitative research, or do you need the reassurance of numbers? Related to this, but slightly more specific, you must ask yourself – do you believe all your company's ads should be tested in exactly the same way? Or will they benefit from research designed around each specific strategy and execution?

If you decide to use one off-the-peg technique – what one researcher called the 'Big Mac' approach – you'll get the advantage of familiarity, a set of norms to make interpretation easier, and everyone in the organisation will know exactly what rules they're playing by.

If you expect tailor-made research for each campaign, it will require a good deal more time and thought on everyone's part. You'll require an experienced advertising researcher who's more interested in solving individual problems than in building up databases (these do exist). It's possible, however, that by doing it this way you'll get better research, and the process of having to design the research to fit the advertisement will itself be valuable in consolidating the thinking behind it.

If you want to commit to one system, as many companies do, then you have to review the evidence and decide which best fits your own beliefs in how advertising works for your company, and your corporate and advertising style. For instance, it may be that if your corporate philosophy is all about product improvements, and the role of advertising is to communicate these, that attitude shift will work for you. If you are more concerned with intangible brand values, you might want to go elsewhere.

It would be a good idea to involve your ad agencies in this decision. You will get better results (and have a nicer time) if you regard copy testing as a process which is meant to help the agency to make better ads, not as an external police force to give them a hard time.

Finally, don't forget that any form of copy testing is only one stage in a successful advertising development process. It's not a substitute for strategic planning and research, and there's usually a role for early developmental research of rough ideas (generally qualitative of course.) No method of copy testing is infallible. Like the little books you can buy at the race course, if it is done well it can read you the form. You can't expect it to tell you what exactly will happen in the race.

# References

Bartos, R. (1986) Founding fathers of advertising research. *Journal of Advertising Research* 26(1), pp. 9–12.

Brown, G. (1991) *How Advertising Affects the Sales of Packaged Goods Brands*. Millward Brown, Leamington Spa.

Farr, A. (1993) Persuasion shift testing – putting the genie back in the bottle. *Admap*, January, pp. 56–63.

Farr, A. & Brown, G. (1994) Persuasion or enhancement? An experiment. Market Research Society conference, Birmingham, March, pp. 69–76.

Feldwick, P. (1992) Headaches and flat feet: a review of current quantitative pre-testing practice. Market Research Society conference, Birmingham, March, pp. 221–230.

Fothergill, J.E. & Ehrenberg, A.S.C. (1965) On the Schwerin analysis of advertising effectiveness. *Journal of Marketing Research* 2, August.

Haley, R.I. & Baldinger, A.L. (1991) The ARF copy research validity project. *Journal of Advertising Research* 31, April/May, pp. 11–32.

Hedges, A. (1974) *Testing to Destruction: a Critical Examination of the Uses of Research in Advertising*. Institute of Practitioners in Advertising, London.

King, S. (1967) Can research evaluate the creative content of advertising? *Admap*, June.

Krugman, H.E. (1977) Memory without recall, exposure without perception. *Journal of Advertising Research* 17(4).

Lodish, L. (1991) The how advertising works project. Proceedings of ARF Key Issues Workshop on Marketplace Advertising Research, New York, November.

Rosenberg, K.E. & Blair, M.H. (1994) The long and short of persuasive advertising. *Journal of Advertising Research* 34(4), pp. 63–69.

Rossiter, J.R. & Eagleson, G. (1994) Conclusions from the ARF's copy research validity project. *Journal of Advertising Research* 34(3), pp. 19–32.

Starch, D. (1923) *Principles of Advertising*. A.W. Shaw Company, Chicago.

Twyman, W.A. (1973) Designing advertising research for marketing decisions. *Journal of the Market Research Society* 38(4).

White, M. (1995) How advertising helped Strepsils to grab a market by the throat. In *Advertising Works 8* (Baker, C., ed.), pp. 375–399. NTC Publications, Henley-on-Thames.

## Afterword

This chapter is simplistic, but every time I have presented it at conferences, members of the audience have come up to me and told me they found it helpful.

The extraordinary thing about pre-testing is how slowly things change. The two fundamental approaches described in this chapter date back to the 1950s and 1960s, and have not really changed much since. The assumptions or 'models' of advertising that underpin them have increasingly been called into question, yet nobody seems to have come up with radical alternatives, and certainly not any that have gained general acceptance. This conservatism is rooted in the organisational needs of both suppliers and users of copy-testing research: both benefit from simple, replicable methods that appear easy to interpret. (There are some excellent researchers who will design research around the strategy for each campaign. Sadly, they rarely become millionaires.)

In fact, if there is a trend in pre-testing it appears to be further consolidation of the biggest systems. This is also driven today by the requirements of multinational brands, for which a standardised global approach has important benefits.

On the other hand, the relevance of methods originally designed specifically for television commercials may be reduced if the traditional TV spot becomes less important in marketing communications. One challenge for advertising research companies will be to design methodologies for evaluating integrated, multi-channel campaigns. Some are certainly looking at this, but it will not be simple.

# Chapter 7

# How Can You Tell if Advertising is Working?

## Introduction

'The time has come when advertising has in some hands reached the status of a science. It is based on fixed principles and is reasonably exact. The causes and effects have been analysed until they are well understood. The correct methods of procedure have been proved and established. We know what is most effective, and we act on basic laws. Advertising, once a gamble, has thus become, under able direction, one of the safest of business ventures.'

Claude Hopkins (1923)

'The effect of most advertising, it should be noted, is as difficult to quantify as, say, the efficacy of prayer... Most advertising efforts go out like acts of faith and hope into silent darkness, producing so little in the way of specific identifiable results that a whole industry has sprung up to provide audience measuring services, and reassurance, and thereby sustain the flagging will.'

Frank Rowsome (1970)

Advertising is an expensive business. Those who spend money on it should want to know what results they're getting. Those who plan and create it should want to find out if what they're doing is working; and how, and why it's working (or not), in order to learn how to do it better next time.

So everyone would like it if the process of evaluating advertising results were simple, precise, and reliable. Unfortunately, it is nearly always none of these. Because of this, people often jump one of two ways. Some are tempted

Reproduced from *How to Plan Advertising* (A. Cooper, ed.), second edition, 1998, by permission of Continuum International Publishing Group Ltd, The Tower Building, York Road, London, UK.

to believe too much; they take results at their face value, which may be misleading, or credit data with a degree of accuracy and reliability that isn't justified. Others become complete sceptics, which is a handy excuse for not bothering with evaluation at all. Both errors have been around for a very long time, and have coexisted quite happily. The literature of advertising is full of quotes stressing the difficulty, or impossibility, of measuring advertising effects, especially on sales. These are counterpointed by a long succession of claims from researchers, ad agencies, and others, that they have at last found 'the answer' to the problem. Such contradictory signals lead to an understandable feeling of uneasiness among advertisers and their agencies – that an ideal answer exists somewhere, or is perhaps just about to exist, but no one is quite sure what or where it is.

Consequently, although there exists a general view that campaign evaluation ought to be a 'good thing', too often little or nothing is actually being done about it. I write this from experience: despite all the breast-beating and all the conferences on the subject, I am still often surprised by how low a priority advertising evaluation often seems to be – both for advertisers *and* for account planners. This is especially true in most markets outside the UK; it is, perhaps surprisingly, largely true in the USA.

Let us start then by saying to all those who feel like this: don't worry about the fact that you have not yet found the Holy Grail. You're not the only ones. In fact, you're right to be confused. There is, for most situations, no solution that is simple, precise and reliable. There is likewise no single solution that is equally suitable for all cases. Evaluating the effects of advertising will involve you in thinking and making judgements – and almost certainly, will cost money.

That's the bad news. The good news is, there is a wide range of possibilities available, and, used intelligently, and often in conjunction with each other, it should be possible to get useful feedback on what is happening as a result of your advertising, and why. The numerous researchers and others who have developed different approaches to advertising evaluation over the last 75 years have each (in most cases anyway) left us with a technique that is useful for *something*. We just have to be a bit wary of frequent overclaims that suggest any of them had a universal or infallible answer. Claude Hopkins, quoted at the head of this chapter, was more right than wrong in the context of mail order advertising, where he had all his experience. His mistake was believing that the same principles would apply to all advertising.

Used thoughtfully, the available techniques for evaluating advertising should always be able to improve the quality and efficiency of your advertising over time. They will increase the chances of killing useless campaigns before it's too late, and just as important, provide evidence to persist with campaigns that *do* work. This is not to say that they will answer all problems, or necessarily 'optimise' anything. But studying how consumers actually respond to advertising in the marketplace is one of the key areas where the account planner can acquire relevant information and understanding.

In order to measure effectiveness, we need to think hard about what sort of effects we expect. What *exactly* will consumers do if they respond to the campaign? What will go on in their minds? What will they need to take from our communications? We need to be very precise about the answers to such questions, and this in itself is a valuable discipline.

## Sales effects vs. consumer effects

There are two basic ways we could define advertising 'effects'. We can look at what happens to *sales* (orders, money changing hands, boxes moving out of shops), or we can look at what happens to *people* who are exposed to the ads: what do they remember, how do their awareness or perceptions or behaviour change? Each of these might be interesting, for different reasons.

Sales, or its equivalent in a non-commercial context, is always the ultimate goal of advertising. It's true that sales may sometimes be influenced by advertising only over the long term, or in conjunction with other activities (which are reasons why we might want to measure other things to isolate an advertising effect in the short term); but in the end the purpose of advertising is to benefit business. In other words, we want to sell more, or more profitably, *with* advertising than we would *without* it.

Consumer responses, on the other hand, can tell us much that sales alone generally can't, about *how* the advertising is (or isn't) working. *Who* is being influenced by the advertising? What are they noticing or remembering about it? How are their perceptions of the brand changing?

However, consumer responses have also often been used to supplement, or even substitute for, sales results, as the ultimate measure of advertising 'success'. Sometimes this is inevitable, because in some categories it is very difficult to get reliable data on consumer sales, or market share; but it is important to remember that consumer responses are all in varying degrees remote from, and not a reliable proxy for, actual sales information. Increases in advertising awareness, or brand awareness, or positive brand attitudes, may all be useful learning, either for diagnostic reasons or if we believe they are 'leading indicators' of a sales response that may take longer to appear, but none of these is the same as a sales response. Listed in Table 7.1 are the commonest measures of 'advertising effect', organised in order of their remoteness from sales.

For many years, influential writers on advertising argued that sales were,

**Table 7.1** Measures of advertising effect.

| Type of advertising effect | Relevant research |
|---|---|
| Exposure to advertising | Media research |
| Recall of advertising | Survey research |
| Attitudes to/communication of advertising | Survey/qualitative research |
| Awareness of brand | Survey research |
| Perceptions/image of brand | Survey/qualitative research |
| Attitude to brand | Survey/qualitative research |
| Claimed consumer behaviour | Survey research |
| Consumer buying behaviour | Panel data |
| Sales | Retail audit, consumer audit, ex-factory data |

for practical purposes, an irrelevant measure of advertising effect. Rosser Reeves (1961) wrote:

'Recently a group of marketing men, almost idly, at a luncheon table, listed thirty seven different factors, any or all of which could cause the total sales of a brand to move up or down.

Advertising was only one of these.

The product may be wrong. Price may be at fault. Distribution may be poor. The sales force may not be adequate. Budget may be too low. A better product may be sweeping the market. A competitor may be outwitting you with strong deals. There are many variables.

And when a wheel has many spokes, who can say which spoke is supporting the wheel?'

Sales responses to advertising *can* be hard to detect, so there is some truth in this, but for many years this had the unfortunate consequence of putting sales results off the evaluation agenda altogether. As a result, it has often been forgotten that all 'intermediate measures' are only valuable in so far as they really are relevant to the behavioural goal of sales; and in evaluating campaigns, as in planning strategy, it is essential to keep this ultimate objective in view at all times.

Therefore sales effects and consumer effects are best seen as complementary, not as alternatives. They give us different kinds of information. They can also be mutually supportive; and each compensates, to some extent, for the other's limitations.

## Relating advertising to sales

The problems of relating advertising to sales, once thought by many to be insuperable, are principally threefold.

Firstly, sales are influenced by many factors other than advertising, so the relationships aren't always clear. Second, sales effects may become fully apparent only over the longer term, while advertisers want short-term indications as to whether the advertising is effective. These are real issues, and they can make it difficult to estimate advertising effects fully or precisely; there are, however, ways of approaching them. But perhaps one should add a third problem, which I have never seen explicitly mentioned but which should be discussed before the others – many advertisers simply don't have good enough sales data to start with.

To look at advertising effects on sales, you normally need something better than just 'ex-factory' sales (though these also have their uses). You want a robust measure, broken down by month or even week, of what the consumer is actually buying, not what is moving into the distribution pipeline.

Many of the 'contaminating factors' that supposedly obscure advertising response – the economy, weather, seasonality, etc. – generally influence all brands on the market alike. It's therefore normally easier to see a relationship between advertising and *share*, than between ads and absolute volumes or values. For this, you need a measure of *total* market sales as well as your own, and (with respect to Rosser Reeves' marketing men over their five-Martini lunch) most short-term variations in share, apart from those caused by advertising, can be explained by movements in *distribution* and relative *price*.

It is in any case very dangerous to look at volume sales or shares as a response to advertising, without taking price into account. Very often, the real business justification for advertising lies not just in increasing or maintaining volumes, but in maintaining a price premium; the importance of margins to profitability is often more crucial than volumes. Any analysis of sales response, therefore, needs to consider prices as well as volumes.

Consequently in order to look for meaningful relationships between advertising and sales, you would ideally want:

- Regular, reliable data on *consumer* sales of *all* the brands in your market
- Price data
- Measures of distribution

In other words, the information you would expect from a retail audit. Now, many advertisers don't have this sort of information! In some cases it's available, but they can't be bothered to pay for it. In many other cases, such data don't even exist. Outside the field of packaged goods, it's probably the rule rather than the exception that robust measurements of markets can't be had, or are incomplete.

Does this mean that sales are an impossible measure after all, for those who are not privileged to have complete data? No – but it's an inescapable

---

**Clarks Desert Boots**

*Clarks ran a campaign for their long-established product, Desert Boots, in the British 'style' press. With a media budget of only £30,000, it clearly wasn't an option to spend any money on research. Nevertheless, a convincing case was made for the effectiveness of the campaign:*

- *Ex-factory sales increased over 500%*
- *Price and distribution remained largely unchanged*
- *A 'no-cost' telephone survey of stockists and a review of advertising-related PR added corroborative evidence that the advertising had made the difference*

*Source:* Advertising Works 5 *(Buck, 1990a)*

---

fact that the more data you have, the more possibilities you have both for precision, and for disentangling complex situations. Sales modelling, for instance, is not an option unless you have a fairly complete data set. Advertising evaluation is the art of the possible.

In a very dynamic situation, you may not need very sensitive data to see a relationship between advertising and sales. If, however, you are looking for more subtle short-term movements, it stands to reason they won't show up without fairly comprehensive data. More important is the fact that if they *don't* show up on *inadequate* data this cannot be used as evidence that the advertising is not effective. It is not unknown for advertising to be blamed for what is really an inadequacy in market measurement. If the sales data available are genuinely inadequate, more emphasis in the evaluation process will inevitably be placed on consumer responses, but this will not make them any more of a substitute for sales data than they would otherwise have been, and their limitations in this respect still need to be remembered.

Whatever you *do* know about sales should always be compared with other sources of data to ensure it is consistent with the overall picture you are hoping to build up. If advertising measures such as awareness and liking are looking good, but your own sales are down, you need to have a theory as to why. Is the advertising at fault, despite some encouraging, but possibly irrelevant, measures? Perhaps the advertising itself is being received as it should, but other factors are causing sales to go down? Each of these possibilities would lead to quite a different set of actions.

The more relevant sales data you have, the more you can do to address the main issue – disentangling the effects of advertising from other marketing factors.

**An unplanned experiment**

*Kia Ora, a fruit drink, was relaunched in the UK with a high-profile advertising campaign and a complete change of packaging, from small glass to large plastic bottles.*

*The increase in sales was substantial – but it was not clear how much this was due to advertising or to the packaging change.*

*It turned out that, due to initial constraints on production, for several months independent grocery stores could not be supplied with the new packs. Special analysis of Nielsen data showed that these stores enjoyed the same increase in sales as others, and that therefore advertising rather than packaging was the driving factor behind the brand's success.*

*Source:* Advertising Works 5 *(Buck, 1990b)*

## Looking at sales data

This begins with visual inspection of the data, relating advertising timing to fluctuations in sales or share. Despite the other factors involved, this often shows a relationship when things are changing quite fast. The relationship then needs to be criticised by looking for, and disposing of, alternative explanations, for example comparing the sales graph with price or distribution movements, or other changes that were known to have taken place.

Visual inspection may give us a reasonable idea that advertising is having an effect, but it is not always very good at putting a value on it. To do this (and to be more certain the effect really exists) we need to have an idea about what *would* have happened without advertising. Often the real justification for advertising is not so much to do with a sales increase, as defending existing business – so the hypothesis has to be that sales would decline without advertising, and might only remain static, or even decline less, with it. There are two ways of estimating this 'might have been' scenario.

### Area tests and controls

The first, which has been used for a long time, is to compare sales in areas with and without advertising (or with different weights of advertising). This can be criticised as rather crude because it depends on the assumption that the two areas are similar in all other respects, which is rarely true. Nevertheless, it is still used, and the results can be convincing, though the problems of measuring and interpreting results are sometimes only discovered after the 'test' has taken place.

### Econometric models

The second approach, which has become much more current in the last 15 years or so, is the application of sales modelling (also known as 'econometrics', 'econometric modelling'or, in the USA, 'market mix modelling').

An econometric model is basically a formula which sets out to explain, or at least describe, variations in a particular line of data: this 'dependent variable', for our purposes, would most likely be a brand's market share or sales. The modeller calculates how the brand's share varies in response to other factors for which data exist, such as relative price, competitive advertising, or the brand's own advertising: these are called the 'independent variables', or sometimes, 'explanatory variables' because they seek to explain the movements in the brand share. The modeller produces a formula which attempts to predict what the brand's share should be, given any combination of values for the explanatory variables. A typical econometric model is shown in the box opposite.

This formula can be used in various ways. It can be used to estimate what would have happened if things had been different; for instance, if the brand had not advertised, how much less its share would have been. (In the boxed example we would just change the value of $A$ and see what happened to $S$.) This offers a very precise estimate of the extent to which extra sales can be attributed to advertising, and so can be related to profit-and-loss accounts.

The model can also be used to predict the future (making certain assumptions), or estimate what future shares would be given different levels of price, advertising, etc., thus helping with future budget planning. One shouldn't get too carried away by this – predicting the future is never *that* easy – but in practice the results of using a sound model are generally much better than guesswork.

Good modelling is a combination of intuition, common sense, trial and error, and a thorough immersion in the relevant statistical theory. This last requirement takes about five years to master and should dissuade the non-econometricians from trying to do it all themselves. The process is not, however, a black box, and good econometricians should be able to explain most of their thinking to the non-expert.

There is not room in a short chapter to do much more than recognise the value of modelling, which I believe will become an increasingly important element of advertising evaluation. It is not, however, without its limitations. In general, models can only 'explain' things within the limits of what has already happened, so they are less reliable when factors such as price differences or advertising budgets move outside this previous range. In addition,

**Anatomy of a model**

$$S = K + aP + bD + cA$$

*Those who are comfortable with maths will see at once what this is getting at. Otherwise, a brief explanation should make it clear.*

*Each letter stands for a number. S might stand for 'sales', or for 'share'. This is the* dependent variable, *the value which the model is attempting to predict.*

*P stands for some measure of price (such as our brand's price indexed on the market average), D for some measure of distribution, A for a measure of advertising input... these are some of the many possible* independent *or* explanatory variables. *In this case, if we know the value of these three for any point in time, we can use the model to estimate what S ought to be for the same period.*

*a, b and c are the numbers by which we have to multiply each of the independent variables to relate them to S. These are called the* parameters.

*K is a* constant, *just a number which we have to add to the rest of the right-hand side of the equation to get the right fit with the thing we are trying to explain.*

*The modeller has three main tasks:*

- *To choose which independent variables will best explain S*
- *To establish the value of the parameters and of K*
- *To ensure that the relationships are meaningful according to statistical tests and to common sense*

*These three tasks are all interrelated, and all involve marketing judgement as well as statistical expertise. Modelling is not (or should not be) a black box; it is an art as well as a science.*

by their nature, models tend to explain *short-term* variations in the data. A model may show why share moves up or down a point or two from month to month, but not why share stays around the 20% mark rather than 15% or 25%. As a result, when advertising is acting over the longer term to maintain brand share around that level, the model may effectively *understate* the effects of advertising. The results of taking this literally can be disastrous. Today's econometricians are working to find ways around this problem, although the underlying issue, stripped of its modelling terminology, is simply that we do not know what might happen to a brand over the long term without advertising, unless we try the experiment. In the meantime we need to remember that what a modeller calls 'advertising effect' may not be the total effect of advertising.

### Measuring sales effects: summary

(1) Always make the attempt to relate advertising to defined sales or business targets.
(2) Get the best data you can on all aspects of market performance.
(3) In particular, consider price as well as volume.
(4) In dynamic situations, sales response to advertising may be fairly easy to see.
(5) Econometric modelling can be used in less obvious situations and to put a more precise value on advertising (but is not infallible).
(6) There is no easy answer to measuring 'long-term effects' in the short term – but some consumer measures may be 'leading indicators'.

## The usefulness of measuring consumer responses to advertising

By 'consumer responses' I am thinking of consumer knowledge, beliefs, attitudes or behaviour that can be measured using survey research or investigated qualitatively. These consumer responses can best be looked at in two categories:

(1) Advertising-related responses
(2) Brand- or other consumer-related responses

### Advertising-related responses

The easiest types of 'effect' to relate to advertising are questions that find out about consumers' reactions to the advertising itself. Did they notice it, or read it? Did they remember it? What did they remember about it? Did they understand it or like it? These reactions can be considered under 'recognition', 'recall', and 'content/message recall'.

#### Recognition or 'reading and noting'
The earliest form of advertising research, other than coupon response, was a measure of ad readership devised by Daniel Starch in the early 1920s (and still used today). This involved taking consumers through an issue of a publication they had read, asking which ads they had noticed and which they read the copy for. This tells us something interesting about an ad – its

ability to attract attention – but it doesn't go very far. (It also turned out to be subject to some error: people would sometimes imagine they had noticed an ad for a product that interested them, when in fact they hadn't.)

### Recall

So a more exacting test of ad effect was devised by George Gallup, which asked people to *remember* (not just recognise) which ads for a product field they had seen. Ever since, asking various forms of recall question has formed one of the staples of advertising research. It is easy to do, it gives a good spread of results, and it seems intuitively likely to most people that remembering an ad should be a necessary precursor of its effectiveness.

While many effective ads are well recalled, this intuitive view can be misleading. We can find examples from both psychology and advertising that suggest advertising *can* work without being consciously recalled. The ad that is better recalled is not necessarily one that is more effective in influencing behaviour; retention in the memory is only one factor contributing to effective advertising.

---

**The answer is 42**

*When we are told the percentage of the population who claim to recall advertising for a brand, it is sometimes difficult to know what to make of it. It may be higher or lower than the figure for competing brands, but is this just because they have spent more or less money? Or were they somehow more famous to start with?*

*To answer such questions Millward Brown developed a modelling technique that explains such a number as a combination of three things:*

*(1) The effect of advertising in the current period.*
*(2) The effect of past advertising.*
*(3) A base level to which advertising recall declines when there is no advertising at all (people often think famous brands have been advertised recently, when in fact they have not).*

*This produces a value they have called the 'Awareness Index', defined as the amount of extra recall that will be created by 100 ratings – so the creative effects of different campaigns can be compared, independent of their weight and timing.*

*This helps us make sense of advertising awareness data. There is still room for debate, however, on how such a measure relates to advertising sales effectiveness.*

There is another danger here, which is also relevant to other types of question asked by survey research. Any advertisement realistically addresses a limited number of the people who have the opportunity to see it. The most extreme example is the classified ad (or many retail ads), which requires only a few individuals, or in some cases only one, to see the ad and respond to it, in order to be a success. At the other extreme, even the most mass market products advertise to only a part of the population. Most products fall along a spectrum between these two extremes. Where ads are addressed to a relatively narrow target audience, therefore, recall (or other) measures based on a broad sample of the population may be largely irrelevant.

---

**Sales without salience?**

*Eurax, an anti-itch cream, was advertised for the first time with a modest budget of £250,000. On a tracking study among all women, spontaneous brand awareness and advertising awareness remained less than 1%. On such measures, the campaign appeared a complete failure.*

*However,* sales *of the brand increased by two-thirds in the quarter following the advertising, and, combined with a price increase, annual revenue for the brand owners went up by 41%. Other factors were involved, but some rudimentary modelling strongly suggested these were not enough to account for the growth.*

*The two findings are not in fact inconsistent. Eurax was a small brand – the extra sales represented about 140,000 packs. Even if each of these was bought by a different woman, this represents only 0.5% of the population.*

*The use of a mass market tracking study may have been inappropriate for a brand on this scale.*

*Source: O'Malley (1991)*

---

In practical terms, this stresses the importance of basing any advertising consumer research on a sample that represents, as far as possible, the target audience – something that is by no means always done and, if the target audience is small, may be very difficult to do without biasing the research. We just have to bear in mind that to measure *numbers* of people recalling the ad (or the brand name, or the message) is not necessarily an indicator of the *strength* of the ad's influence on the individuals who did respond to it in some way.

### Content recall, attitudes to ad

As well as measuring ad recognition or recall, surveys can ask about message recall, comprehension, or attitudes to the ad (e.g. liking, irritation, usefulness, etc.). Such questions promise useful diagnostic information about reactions to the ad, and the appeal of asking them on a tracking study is that it measures response in the 'real world', rather than a laboratory situation.

However, unless recall of the ad is particularly high, this can be a difficult and expensive method of finding how people responded to the ad. If, on a sample of 500, only 10% remember seeing it at all (not a very low figure), this leaves only an absolute maximum of 50 who can then be asked more detailed questions about it. So despite the artificiality of the viewing situation, a great deal more diagnostic information can be gathered more cheaply by using some form of 'impact and communication' test. This kind of research is useful as part of a campaign tracking procedure, as well as in a 'go/no-go' pre-testing situation.

## Brand-related or other consumer-related responses

These types of responses are most commonly divided into: brand awareness, either spontaneous or prompted; brand image or perceptions (i.e. a range of attributes); and overall attachment to or rating of the brand (including the brand size effect and the frequency with which change needs to be monitored).

### Brand awareness

Brand awareness is always easy to measure, but not always very relevant. For some situations, spontaneous awareness is important – I have a need, I think of a name in response to it, and the 'salience' of one brand name over another gives it a greater chance of getting the business. In these cases it is also important to specify the correct 'trigger'.

---

**The appropriate trigger for brand recall**

*A US brand, Liquid Plumr (a product for unblocking drains), defined their competitive set as not just other drain cleaning products, but all drain unblocking services.*

*The appropriate question to measure the salience of Liquid Plumr was therefore not*

*'What drain cleaning products can you think of?', but*
*'What would you do if you had a blocked drain?'*

In many other cases, spontaneous awareness is not so obviously important. In a lot of purchases we are choosing from a range of alternatives displayed before us, not searching for a name we have already thought of. It is true that in most such situations, even if we know nothing much about the brands on offer, we normally tend to choose one we have heard of over one we have never heard of.

---

**When brand awareness is important**

*When buying a life policy or pension through an independent broker, customers are offered a choice of two or three brands which have already been objectively selected, by the broker, to suit their needs. It is therefore very difficult for them to make a further selection on 'rational' grounds.*

*Research showed very clearly, however, that people would always choose a familiar brand over a less familiar one. For Scottish Amicable it was estimated that if advertising could increase prompted name awareness, it would lead to an increase in acceptance and so in sales.*

*A new campaign in 1991 increased brand awareness from 40% to 60% with a resulting 15% increase in sales.*

*Source:* Advertising Works 7 *(Storey, 1993)*

---

For established brands in big markets, however, prompted awareness is not a very useful discriminator as the figure is likely to be above 90%.

There is, to confuse the matter a little more, also some evidence that the ability to think of a name spontaneously is an indicator of positive feelings about the brand. But not infallibly so: we can all think of very famous names which are famous for negative reasons. If this is the purpose of the questions, therefore, we need some more direct evidence of brand attitude as well as mere 'top of mindness'.

### Brand image and attitude

There is no room in this chapter to describe the range of techniques that exist, qualitative as well as quantitative, for attempting to measure the beliefs and associations of various kinds that consumers may have for different brands, and which I still prefer to lump together under the overall name of 'brand image'. Nor the equally wide range of approaches that can be taken to measuring overall brand attitude or 'brand strength'.

The relevance of these kinds of measures, and the exact formulation of them, should depend on the kind of mental process by which advertising is expected to work. Some campaigns are intended to influence behaviour by communicating information, others by changing the context or associations people have for the brand. Questions can be designed to check whether these communications have been effective. In other cases, advertising may work by reminding them of things they already know, or making the brand name more top of mind; here, brand image-type measures may not be very relevant to advertising effect.

### Rating of the brand
There are two general points to be made that apply to this kind of measure. One is the effect of brand size in making sense of the data. The other is the frequency with which these things need to be monitored.

*The brand size effect*: This is most simply illustrated by a simple example, as below.

|  | Cornflakes (%) | All Bran (%) |
| --- | --- | --- |
| Q: Which of these brands would you say tastes nice? | 64 | 10 |

It would be easy, looking at this, to conclude something like: 'Cornflakes is obviously a stronger brand than All Bran on "Tastes nice". There's a clear goal for advertising to persuade people that All Bran tastes as good as Cornflakes'.

However, what in fact happens is that bigger brands in a category (which essentially means brands bought by more people) tend to get rated more highly or on more attributes by more people. Such patterns therefore don't add anything much to our knowledge that Cornflakes is a bigger brand than All Bran.

|  | Cornflakes (%) | All Bran (%) |
| --- | --- | --- |
| Tastes nice | 64 | 10 |
| Easy to digest | 60 | 19 |
| Popular with all the family | 61 | 5 |
| The kind you come back to | 65 | 4 |
| Reasonably priced | 59 | 5 |
| Average | 62 | 9 |
| Buy regularly | 48 | 7 |

Abridged from Barwise & Ehrenberg (1985)

This pattern doesn't explain away all the variation in the data (if it did, the survey wouldn't tell us anything useful), but what is significant is the way that individual figures differ from what would be expected, e.g. All Bran is clearly higher than expected here on 'easy to digest'. There are various ways of looking for this: by graphing, or by looking at how each figure varies from the average; or by analysing perceptions by users of each brand.

This 'brand size effect' is fairly well known, but it has a further implication for advertising evaluation. If a brand's share goes up, we'd naturally expect to see more people rating it on image attributes. To see these figures move up doesn't necessarily tell us much about advertising effect. If, however, the brand moves more strongly on some dimensions than others – say, something featured in the advertising strategy – it adds to the evidence that advertising was influencing the sales movements.

*How often do we need to measure change?* The type of questions described in this section are perhaps most familiar today as constituting the ingredients of 'tracking studies'. This name has been used to describe any research repeated over time, whether the interval be annual, or weekly, as in the continuous tracking studies that have become popular in recent years.

Different frequencies of conducting research have different pros and cons. For monitoring advertising response, annual (or even quarterly) surveys have disadvantages – they may fall shortly after, or a long time after, the last burst of advertising, making comparisons of the results over time almost impossible to read. Because of this, 'pre and post' surveys are more often used, where timing draws a clear contrast between the before and after, or ensures that waves of research are at an equal distance in time from the advertising.

In many ways, therefore, the ideal would be a continuous tracking study which monitors every peak and trough of response. Many clever things can be done with continuous tracking studies, but they are extremely expensive, requiring huge amounts of fieldwork. Apart from possibly using up a disproportionate share of the research budget, this cost factor can easily lead to compromise on length and quality of questionnaire. To measure brand image sensitively requires in most cases a longer questionnaire than is possible on the average continuous tracking study.

It also happens that measures of brand image, if they are meaningful, generally move rather slowly; in fact, the only type of consumer response that consistently moves rapidly and in obvious response to advertising, is advertising recall. It is therefore questionable how cost-effective it is to monitor brand image or brand attitudes on a continuous basis. It might be more sensible in many cases to conduct a more in-depth study of brand perceptions and usage, every year, or even every other year.

The question of how often to 'track' responses to advertising needs to be considered individually for each case, taking into account how quickly relevant responses are expected to change, and how much money is realistically available for the task. If the price of continuous tracking means that the brand will have to do without reliable market data or sales modelling, or proper in-depth understanding of consumer usage and attitudes, it is probably not worth it.

## Claimed behaviour

In some cases tracking studies, or 'pre and posts', need to include questions about usage of the product, because reliable sales data don't exist. Asking such questions can also tell us who is buying what (not apparent from the normal retail audit), and is in any case needed in order to cross-analyse the data by brand usage, etc.

Claimed behaviour may go beyond simple purchasing. It may be used to estimate new trial. Sometimes advertising works by encouraging a particular type of usage, such as the Hellmann's mayonnaise campaign.

---

**Changing usage behaviour**

*Prior to advertising, mayonnaise was seen by the UK consumer as a dressing for salads, which considerably limited its potential for growth. A new campaign for Hellmann's based on the line 'Don't save it for the salad' encouraged usage in many other situations, leading to a trebling of the mayonnaise sector over three years. One measure of advertising effect was the number of consumers using Hellmann's in ways other than on salad.*

*Source:* Advertising Works 3 *(Feldwick, 1985)*

---

So such questions are often important, even though we know that claimed behaviour is generally a less reliable guide to actual behaviour than panel data.

## Consumer response: summary

(1) Measures of advertising recognition and recall can be useful, but despite their popularity they are not measures of advertising 'effectiveness'.
(2) In-depth information about advertising response may be more cost-effectively gathered in a laboratory-style test than in a tracking study.
(3) 'Intermediate measures' should be selected to fit our expectations of how the advertising should influence behaviour, e.g. by factual communication, or name awareness, or imagery.
(4) Measures of brand awareness are sometimes highly relevant and sometimes largely irrelevant, depending on the nature of the purchase decision.
(5) Numbers of respondents rating a brand on any attribute tend to vary with the brand's numbers of users, and this needs to be taken into account when interpreting the data.

(6) Brand image and attitude tend to move slowly, and an in-depth study every year or two may be more valuable than the attempt to track continuously.

(7) Claimed behaviour is useful either as a surrogate for proper market data, or to measure other aspects of changing behaviour, or as a cross-break for analysis.

## Indirect effects of advertising

Everything written so far is implicitly about the 'direct' effects of advertising on the consumer, but it is important to remember that advertising often works in other ways, by influencing employees, the retail trade, or journalists. The significance of these effects is often ignored, but they must be taken into account when evaluating a campaign.

## A note on consumer panels and 'single source'

Consumer panels to some extent straddle the two categories of 'sales' and 'consumer'. Panels are often used to monitor aggregate market share data and can provide much the same information as a retail audit, including price, though not distribution, and therefore can be analysed or modelled in a similar way. They also provide information not available from a retail audit. They can measure, for instance, levels of trial and repeat purchase, and patterns of brand switching, all of which might be very relevant to evaluating certain campaigns. In addition they can tell us who is buying, or among which demographic groups sales increases are happening.

There has been a lot of work done recently in the USA and in Europe on 'single-source' panels; these are panels where both purchasing behaviour and media exposure are measured for the same sample of respondents (Jones, 1995). As this is expensive and difficult to do, a practical alternative which is also available is to produce a similar database by 'fusing' together a separate purchasing panel with a media exposure panel, such as AGB Superpanel with BARB. In both cases, this offers the opportunity to relate ad viewing to brand choice at every level from the individual upwards.

The apparent potential in single-source panels for a new, more precise and informative means of evaluating sales response to advertising has excited a number of people. However, the sheer quantity of data that such systems create, while tantalisingly offering the answers to many problems, makes the best mode of analysis a far from straightforward matter. The area is currently, therefore, somewhat dogged with controversy which there is not space, nor perhaps a pressing need, to enter into here. For our immediate purpose –

which is a brief practical guide to techniques readily available today – we may conclude that at the time of writing, 'single source' is still at a somewhat experimental stage as a practical tool for advertising evaluation. Proper single-source panels are immensely costly, and are therefore not easily available, though fusion may be a way of getting round this. While all this may change, single source is not at present the Holy Grail of advertising research, whatever its enthusiasts may say.

## Conclusions: putting it all together

It was stated at the outset that there is no single simple and reliable way to measure advertising effect. The best approach is to measure more than one level of effect in order to build an overall picture of how consumers are responding to a campaign. This should always involve looking at sales, as far as possible, as well as different measures of consumer response (and being alert to indirect effects as well).

The secret of campaign evaluation is selecting and designing measures which reflect the objectives and the strategy of the campaign. If the objective of the advertising is essentially maintenance, or price enhancement, it is pointless to look for short-term leaps in volume; there is no reason why a niche brand with a 1% market share should want to double its spontaneous awareness among a broad target market of all category users. It is a matter of thinking, not of applying universal formulae; apart from certain less obvious pitfalls (the main ones having been mentioned in this chapter), advertising evaluation does largely depend on imagination and common sense.

To end this chapter, and pull together some principles already suggested, I describe an outline review process recently introduced into DDB around the world. It is called the 'Evaluation and Learning Process': because the most important purpose of evaluation is learning for the future.

## Evaluation and learning process

### What did we expect to happen?

Be clear about what this particular campaign was meant to achieve, and how it was expected to work:

- Overall business objective, e.g. maintenance, growth, price (quantified)
- Target audience
- Desired action – where in the purchase decision process did we want to influence consumer behaviour?

- How the advertising was expected to influence the consumer: e.g. awareness, notoriety, attractiveness, information…

### What did happen?

Review the best evidence we can get about what happened:

- To sales
- To the consumer
- To other parties (retailers, competitors)
- And what else was going on in the world: new products, the weather, health scares, etc.

### Isolate the effect of advertising from other factors

Does it look as if the advertising worked?

- Then: are we confident it was the advertising and not something else?
- Play devil's advocate!

or,

Does it look as if the advertising didn't work?

- Were the objectives unrealistic?
- Did other events interfere with what we were trying to do? or
- Was the advertising at fault?

### Diagnose reasons for failure (and for success)

- Strategic reasons: e.g. wrong choice of target audience, misunderstanding of consumer motivations, buying decisions, etc.
- Executional reasons: ad not linked with the brand name, alienating people, misunderstood, etc.
- Media/budget: outspent or simply not spending enough

### What have we learnt from the experience?
### What should we do next?

Open-ended questions! – which naturally lead back to the start of the advertising planning cycle. Advertising evaluation is not just the end of the story, but should also be a new beginning.

# References

Barwise, P. & Ehrenberg, A.S.C. (1985) Consumer beliefs and brand usage. *Journal of the Market Research Society* 27(2).

Buck, A. (1990a) Clarks' Desert Boots. In *Advertising Works 5* (Feldwick, P., ed.), pp. 234–243. Cassell, London.

Buck, A. (1990b) Going for the heart of a market – Kia Ora orange squash 1983–86. In *Advertising Works 5* (Feldwick, P., ed.), pp. 97–119. Cassell, London.

Feldwick, P. (1985) The respositioning of Hellmann's Mayonnaise. In *Advertising Works 3* (Channon, C., ed.), pp. 84–104. Holt, Rinehart & Winston, London.

Hopkins, C. (1923) *Scientific Advertising*. NTC Business Books, Lincolnwood, Illinois.

Jones, J.P. (1995) *When Ads Work*. Lexington Books, New York.

O'Malley, D. (1991) Sales without salience? Small brands, advertising models – and the curse of television. *Admap*, September.

Reeves, R. (1961) *Reality in Advertising*. Alfred A. Knopf, New York.

Rowsome, F. (1970) *Think Small. The Story of Those Volkswagen Ads*. The Stephen Greene Press, Brattleboro, Vermont.

Storey, R. (1993) Scottish Amicable – how it paid to be amicable. In *Advertising Works 7* (Baker, C., ed.), pp. 333–358. NTC Publications, Henley-on-Thames.

# Further reading (including more recent publications)

There is a huge literature relating to the topic of advertising evaluation. I have kept this list as short as possible; anyone who wants to go further will find plenty of references in the first three titles mentioned.

Jones, J.P. (1986) *What's in a Name? Advertising and the Concept of Brands*. Lexington Books, Massachusetts.

Broadbent, S. (1989) *The Advertising Budget*. NTC Publications in association with the Advertising Association, Henley-on-Thames.

Broadbent, S. (1997) *Accountable Advertising*. Admap Publications in association with the ISBA and the IPA, Henley-on-Thames.

Broadbent, S. (1999) *When to Advertise*. Admap Publications in association with the ISBA and the IPA, Henley-on-Thames.

Heath, R. (2001) *The Hidden Power of Advertising: How Low Involvement Processing Influences the Way We Choose Brands*. Admap Publications, Henley-on-Thames.

McDonald, C. (1992) *How Advertising Works*. NTC Publications in association with the IPA, Henley-on-Thames.

The last book is the best short overview of this perplexing subject, an understanding of which is closely bound up with questions of evaluation

The 11 volumes of *Advertising Works* (since Volume 6, published by NTC Publications/World Advertising Research Center with the IPA), including the introductions, are also invaluable as resources.

The most useful (and readable) journal is *Admap* from the World Advertising Research Center, in which the issues raised in this chapter have been regularly debated for the past 30 years. It is probably the most effective way of keeping up to date with new developments in the field.

## Afterword

New papers, conferences and books on campaign evaluation continue to arrive all the time. The most interesting debates, which I will touch on in my final chapter, involve challenging our basic assumptions about how advertising works – a subject that ultimately underlies the problems of evaluation. But today, at a practical level, I believe the basic menu of approaches is still pretty much as described in this chapter.

What is still surprising is how little both agencies and advertisers seem to interest themselves, on an everyday basis, in campaign evaluation. There is even a widespread and dangerous mind-set in many marketing departments that 'the past' (even the last few years) is irrelevant, and that spending time on it distracts from being 'future-oriented' – though how anyone can anticipate or plan for the future without understanding the past is never explained. To obtain even a few years' continuous back-data on market performance (essential for sales modelling) in the average marketing company is harder than studying medieval history, and even the big data providers themselves, I am told, routinely wipe all their tapes when they are three years old. (This failure to archive information is one very practical reason why preparing a case for the IPA Effectiveness Awards can be so time-consuming, and hence one factor in the continued decline in entries for that excellent competition.)

At a recent meeting convened at the London Business School to discuss advertising effectiveness, those advertisers who were present (only a few of those invited) generally expressed more interest in the subject of pre-testing than in campaign evaluation. Perhaps, if shareholder value analysis leads to finance departments taking more of an interest in measuring marketing effectiveness, this attitude will change. Tim Ambler (2000, p. 11) has actually suggested that responsibility for evaluating marketing should lie with the finance director – but that would be a big cultural shift.

### Reference
Ambler, T. (2000) *Marketing and the Bottom Line*. FT/Prentice Hall, London.

# Chapter 8
# Is Advertising Science or Art?

## Introduction and history

In 1901 Walter Dill Scott, a professor of psychology at Northwestern University, accepted an invitation to address the Agate Club of Chicago, an association of prominent businessmen (and yes, in those days you can bet they were men). His subject was 'The psychology of involuntary attention as applied to advertising'. The talk was a success. Scott was invited back to give a series of lectures on the psychology of advertising, which were later published in a magazine and appeared in 1903 as a book *The Psychology of Advertising* – probably the first, but by no means the last book on this subject by an academic. The work is dedicated to 'that increasing number of *American businessmen* who successfully apply science where their predecessors were confined to custom'.

Despite the obvious interest in his talks, Scott's appearance was not without controversy. Many of his colleagues strongly disapproved of him sullying his academic reputation in this rather shady side of the business world. On the other hand, there were those within the advertising profession itself who were sceptical of his scientific approach. One writer in *Printer's Ink*, the trade magazine of the time, wrote that good advertising depended on 'good judgement, good taste, good ideas, and a whole lot of other good things that could not be dissected or classified by the college professor'. Another argued that 'the attempt to reduce advertising's influence to a science is futile' (Schultze, 1983).

Almost a hundred years ago, I feel, some battle lines were already being drawn here. On the one hand were the ancestral claims of the world of 'art' to own advertising – its roots in the use of language and the craft of illustration, its dependence on 'good judgement, good taste, and other good things'. On the other were the powerful new claims made by academia, speaking for the world of scientific enquiry, its claims to understand the workings of the human mind and explain the roots of social behaviour. Art and science were fighting for the affections of a third party, business, which is represented in my imagination by a member of the Agate Club of Chicago – a large businessman with a walrus moustache and a fat cigar. Now business is not, as a rule, very comfortable with art, but in reality it has only slightly greater a regard for science. Business is mainly interested in customers, sales, above all in money, and it will tolerate art or science only as long as either can promise, in a way it can understand, to deliver these. Science, because it uses numbers, has a marginally greater hold on the business world's affections.

One powerful dynamic in the history of advertising thought is to consider the ways in which these three meta-models of the world – art, science and business – have interacted, fought, argued, and for too much of the time, basically misunderstood each other. I will be giving no secrets away if I admit right now that in my view success in advertising depends on acceptance of all three realities. My purpose in this final chapter is to sketch out how these three worlds have related to each other since the days of Professor Scott at the Agate Club, and to explore some of the ways art, science and business have ignored or denigrated each other, or more subtly, borrowed each other's garments.

As advertising in the USA boomed, along with the economy, in the years before and after the First World War, it became associated with two relatively new and fashionable schools of thought. One was the recently emergent science of psychology. Most of what we would now recognise as psychology dates from the 1880s, or later. One of the earliest fields subject to psychological experiment was memory, as studied by Ebbinghaus, and this was a strong influence on the early application of psychology to advertising in the hands of two young and entrepreneurial college professors from the mid-west, Daniel Starch and George Gallup.

The other was the movement towards 'efficiency' as in the famous time-and-motion studies of Frederick W. Taylor, who discovered that measurement itself was a powerful instrument of control and thus of getting improved returns on investment.

Both these themes had a strong influence on advertising practice during this period. Efficiency came first, through the development of the split run and its near miraculous ability to measure and therefore increase the efficiency of direct response advertising. 'Mail order advertising' became the test bed for any agency to hone its craft and establish its quasi-scientific credentials. Theory quickly followed practice. Because the mail order ad was the type of ad whose efficiency could be measured, so it became the model for every successful ad; in all models of advertising created around this period, and which are still with us, the final step in success is always 'a sale' (not 'a repeat purchase', a 'loyal customer', a 'strong brand', or even 'an increased disposition to buy'). The copywriter John E. Kennedy famously formalised this in the phrase which won him his highly paid job at Lord and Thomas. As the story goes, the unknown Kennedy sent up to Albert Lasker, the boss of the agency, a note that read 'If you will give me ten minutes of your time, I can tell you what advertising is'. His definition was 'advertising is salesmanship in print', and Lasker was so impressed he hired him on the spot (Gunther, 1960, p. 57).

This theme was developed and made universally known by another Lord and Thomas writer, Claude Hopkins, who in 1923 published the best selling advertising book of all time, *Scientific Advertising*. The title (perhaps deliberately echoing that of Frederick Taylor's (1911) book, *The Principles of Scientific Management*), was a clever choice. Hopkins, who was nothing if not a brilliant copywriter, instinctively understood that science, not art, was the way to the hearts of the business community, and the famous opening paragraph offers total certainty, based on a myth of objective science:

> 'The time has come when advertising has in some hands reached the status of a science. It is based on fixed principles and is reasonably exact. The causes and effects have been analysed until they are well understood. The correct methods of procedure have been proved and established. We know what is most effective, and we act on basic laws. Advertising, once a gamble, has thus become, under able direction, one of the safest of business ventures.'
>
> (Hopkins, 1923, pp. 57–58)

Yet *Scientific Advertising* contains not a single number, nor a reference to any empirical evidence or experiments. It contains no acknowledgement of the psychological theories of Scott, or of anyone else. 'Science' is here a smokescreen for Hopkins' own practical experience, both as a salesman and a copywriter. Yet the claim was enough to give Hopkins' rules for good advertising a credibility and a currency that it would be impossible to overestimate.

For certain advertising tasks, most clearly but not exclusively mail order advertising, Hopkins' rules still make a great deal of sense (and many people in ad agencies today unfairly disparage them). The key issue, of course, is whether these principles, arrived at by trial and error for mail order ads, hold true for ads that are not mail order. Scientifically it is hard to show why they should – but the equation of advertising with 'salesmanship' had gone so far, and so many people had a vested interest in wanting it to be true , that it was widely assumed to be so. Hopkins wrote: 'Advertising does not exist to keep your name before the public. It does not exist to help your other salesmen'.

Yet he never said why not, and in fact a vast amount of advertising both before and after Hopkins did, and does, exist precisely in order to do these things. The problem is that the efficiency of this kind of advertising is far harder to measure.

Meanwhile, the psychology professors were coming at the issue of efficiency from another angle. Starch had begun with coupon response, but found increasingly clients were asking for a similar type of measure for non-coupon ads. He addressed this by positing a model of advertising which has formed the basis for most others ever since. Starch's model states that to be successful an ad must be *noticed – read – understood – remembered – acted upon* (Starch, 1923). Like other so-called 'hierarchical' advertising models, Starch's has a strong intuitive appeal – it looks like 'common sense'. Starch focused on the first two steps of this hierarchy, and adapted a method of measuring reading and noting which he had previously used in studying newspaper readership patterns.

However, there is a sleight of hand in this logic. The hierarchical model makes sense only in the 'salesmanship' or direct response situation. And yet it was precisely for non-mail order ads that the system was being devised! Focusing on the first steps of the hierarchy – the wide end of the funnel – creates a serious nonsense, because it does not follow that maximising the numbers of people noticing or reading an ad is equivalent to maximising the numbers who will ultimately be influenced by it. Most mail order ads need to attract the attention of only a very small number of people – those who are actively in the market for the product, and therefore disposed to action. Reading and noting scores for direct response ads are pointless, yet by setting up what was to become the 'Starch rating' as the all-important measure of advertising success, Starch immediately created a totally different set of criteria for creating ads. John Caples, another great copywriter in the mail order tradition, was scathing about Starch ratings. Agencies, he said, have an easy way to beat that game: 'Instead of showing a big picture of the car, you show a big picture of Marilyn Monroe and a little picture of the car. If that doesn't work, you take some clothes off her' (Mayer, 1958, p. 249).

Gallup followed Starch by developing an alternative methodology based on recall rather than recognition, which led to a powerful tradition of using recall as the key measure of advertising success that still dominates much thinking today. Though different in some ways from Starch ratings, recall also makes the same underlying (and questionable) assumption – that the more people remember an ad, the more will be influenced by it.

Thus developed two, largely incompatible, models of advertising. The first based on the idea of 'salesmanship', with a set of rules based on Hopkins: verbal; informational ('the more you tell, the more you sell'); distrustful of humour or any kind of eccentricity; and totally focused on the few 'prospects' in the target market. The other based on measures of recognition or recall – which, paradoxically, incentivised the writers of ads to use irrelevant visuals, humour, and just the kind of eccentricity Hopkins so deplored. In a strange way both models became established as part of the orthodoxy, and both claimed 'science' as their justification. If ad agency people tried to call either model into question, they would be firmly put in their place as self-indulgent 'artists' who must submit to the superiority of scientific learning.

In fact, neither model could have stood up for long to the scrutiny of whether or not it was science. A true scientific enquiry into how advertising works could have shown them up years ago. But nobody was doing this, least of all in the academic world. Since Scott's day, advertising courses have proliferated in US universities. Vast numbers of professors and lecturers have studied the subject. Yet, remarkably few seem to have effectively challenged the status quo they inherited. Such challenges as there have been to orthodox thinking are as likely to have come from a thoughtful person with practical industry experience, a Herb Krugman or a Timothy Joyce, as from academia. The academics, most of whom had no real experience of creating ads, generally had no incentive to question what they were being taught. The dominant paradigm, for all its internal contradictions, held firm.

Yet, many people who worked in advertising, who believed they had some insight into how to write ads that would touch people's hearts and minds, were continually frustrated by the narrow models imposed on them. The 'sales' model and the 'recall' model are clearly incompatible, but in part they managed to coexist by emphasising the things they appeared to have in common. One was Starch's original hierarchical model, another was an emphasis on the verbal rather than the visual. Hopkins had distrusted pictures and argued for long copy; message recall measures invariably favoured ideas that could be put into words. Together, these reinforced a model of advertising as 'salesmanship working by rational persuasion' which came to dominate advertising orthodoxy.

We can trace a number of attacks on the orthodoxy which had some measure of success. However, one might say they all ultimately failed, at least in dislodging the rational, hierarchical model from the heartland of corporate America. I will deal with three.

## Motivation in advertising

The first was the interest during the 1950s in what was then known as 'motivational research'. In order to assault the mock scientific barricades, art would not be enough – the attackers needed their own kind of science. They found it in Freudian psychoanalysis, and particularly in some of the Viennese refugees who came to the USA after the First World War, such as Dr Ernest Dichter. Most people today agree Dichter wasn't a very good researcher. He largely ignored his data, such as they were. He was, however, an extremely insightful and creative thinker. He would have made a great account planner, or indeed a creative. His particular *shtick* was to realise that corporate America would be much more receptive to his ideas if they were dressed up as Freudian 'science'.

In 1957 a journalist from Chicago, Pierre Martineau, wrote a book called *Motivation in Advertising*. Martineau used theories of Freudian analysis dressed up as 'motivation' to legitimise all the things that the dominant models ignored – emotions, the power of visuals, the use of humour, the role of creativity. It's a fine book, long out of print and little known today.

In the same year another journalist, Vance Packard, wrote a more famous book, *The Hidden Persuaders*. Using a carefully crafted combination of innocent truths, sinister sounding half-truths and the occasional downright fiction, Packard created a vision of an advertising industry manipulating the subconscious of every citizen for mysterious ends. Packard touched a raw nerve. This was the era of the Cold War – captured American soldiers in Korea were known to have been subjected to the ancient Chinese art of *Hsi Nao* ('wash-brain') to turn them into communists. Did advertising work in a similar way, by brainwashing people?

Suddenly, it seemed, nobody wanted to know about 'motivations' any more. Corporate America wanted a return to the simple certainties of salesmanship, the honest pitch of the travelling preacher and the snake oil salesman (both, incidentally, previous careers of Claude Hopkins). An astute agency boss, Rosser Reeves, produced a book in 1961 whose title positions it as a deliberate rejoinder to Martineau and the motivation school. He called it *Reality in Advertising*. In Chapter 19, The Freudian Hoax, he wrote: 'There are no hidden persuaders. Advertising works openly, in the bare and pitiless sunlight.' In Reeves' book, emotions, visuals, 'brand image', are all ideas damned with faint praise. All very well in their way, but if you really want to *sell*, what you need is a USP – a Unique Selling Proposition.

With a sigh of relief lots of people went back to business as before, although at least one man continued quietly fighting his corner for 'good taste and all the other good things'. One can hardly say he failed; *Advertising Age* in 1999 voted him the most influential ad person of the twentieth century. And yet it is possible that some of his success came at the expense of widening the split between 'art' and 'science' in advertising. His name was William Bernbach.

# William Bernbach

Bernbach was originally a political speechwriter, and schooled in the art of rhetoric. (If we were to go into the history of rhetoric we would find that even in the time of the ancient Greeks, there were stand-offs between those who believed that great speeches had to conform to rules and those who believed they were a matter for individual inspiration: see, for example, Plato's *Phaedrus*). He went into advertising with the Grey agency, and left it in 1949 when he worried it was getting big and becoming too hide-bound by rules. Just before resigning, he wrote in a letter:

> 'I'm worried that we're going to fall into the trap of bigness, that we're going to worship techniques instead of substance. I don't want academicians. I don't want scientists. I don't want people who do the right things. I want people who do inspiring things...'

Bernbach was a charismatic leader. He hardly ever wrote ads himself, but he created an agency where the best people all desperately wanted to write ads for him. And he then knew how to give his clients the courage and conviction to run with them. He never wrote a book, but frequently gave interviews or wrote short articles throughout his career. His own creative skills live on in the phrases he found to justify his own point of view, including the following:

> 'There are a lot of great technicians in advertising... They know all the rules. They can tell you that people in an ad will get you greater readership. They can tell you that a sentence should be this short or that long. They can tell you that body copy should be broken up for easier and more inviting reading. They can give you fact after fact after fact. They are the scientists of advertising. But there's one little rub. Advertising is fundamentally persuasion, and persuasion happens to be not a science, but an art'

> (Bernbach, 1980).

As Bernbach pointed out, artistry is a characteristic of all good advertising – and that includes mail order. Even Hopkins' own reputation must have been based on more than just following rules – or else, surely, Lord and Thomas would have been crazy to pay him $300,000 a year. John Caples' most famous ad, which ran and ran for years in the 1920s and 1930s, was for a correspondence course in playing the piano. It arrested the reader with the headline: 'They laughed when I sat down at the piano. But when I started to play...' Bill Bernbach commented:

> 'What if this ad had been written in a different language? Would it have been as effective? What if it had said, "They admired my piano playing", which also plays

to the instinct of being admired? Would that have been enough? Or was it the talented, imaginative expression of the thought that did the job? That wonderful feeling of revenge... Suppose Winston Churchill had said "We owe a lot to the RAF" instead of "Never was so much owed by so many to so few". Do you think the impact would have been the same? Suppose David Ogilvy had said in his Rolls Royce ad: "The quietest car in the world" instead of "At 60 miles an hour the loudest noise you hear is the clock". Would that have been the same? Would you even have believed it?'

Towards the end of his life, Bernbach became interested in psychology and spent a lot of time with the Sirk Institute in California, but he was not a scientist, and never really articulated a successful scientific theory behind what he did. In a way it was impossible he should do so. He fell back on phrases like 'the passion', 'unchanging human nature', ideas which, as he said, went back as far as Aristotle – but which lacked the measurability that the positivist schools demanded. He is most widely remembered today as an inspiring and pragmatic creative leader, rather than as a theorist – and if he was not exactly anti-research, he clearly regarded it as having a fairly humble role.

## The British account planning movement

There were a number of people working in advertising in London in the 1960s who shared Bill Bernbach's frustration with the way things were done, but were prepared to give research, and indeed genuine science, a bigger role. Pre-eminent among these were Stephen King, Timothy Joyce, Judie Lannon and others at the London office of J Walter Thompson, and Stanley Pollitt of Pritchard Wood and Partners, later Boase Massimi Pollitt (Pollitt, 2001). They felt convinced that the hierarchical, rational models of advertising, and their associated research techniques, had got it all wrong, but also believed that a more genuinely scientific theory of how advertising worked and a more intelligent and open-minded use of research should help their case.

One *locus classicus* for this movement is Timothy Joyce's 1967 ESOMAR paper, 'What do we know about how advertising works?'. Joyce brought together empirical evidence from a number of sources to suggest that much advertising works in a way that Starch and the early writers had never considered. He quoted hard behavioural analysis of purchasing behaviour from Andrew Ehrenberg which showed that people are repertoire buyers and not loyalists who 'switch'. He looked at more recent psychological theories such as Festinger's theory of 'cognitive dissonance' and even Gestalt psychology. Perhaps wisely, the original planners stayed away from the wilder shores of Freud, but made extensive use (often unacknowledged) of a paper written by two of the American 'motivation researchers' of the 1950s (Gardner & Levy, 1955), in elaborating a theory of brands which was central to their model of advertising effect.

Rather than persuading people by rational argument to switch from Brand A to Brand B, advertising insinuates (often unconsciously) memories and associations into people's minds about a brand which in minor ways may influence their choice at some future time. The business pay-off of advertising generally comes in the longer term with the cumulative effects of these minor influences both on behaviour patterns and on perceptions. Advertising does as much to reinforce behaviour after the event as to create it.

The practical implications of this thinking were seen in the UK, at first in their own agencies. Research, including qualitative research, was used to understand the target group and inform creative work, not just to make decisions between one idea and another. There was an emphasis on copy testing, but as qualitative feedback on an execution rather than as a predictor of sales. There was an emphasis on managing the brand as a whole, not just looking at each ad in isolation. Later, there was a body of research into measuring actual campaign effectiveness (the IPA Advertising Effectiveness Awards) which showed repeatedly that the sort of ads that really did achieve market success were very often closer to the creative world view than the orthodox one.

Yet none of these initiatives, though they caused considerable disruption to the status quo, ever managed to bridge the gap between the world of science and the world of art. They implied, but never quite demonstrated why, effective persuasive communications are produced in the final analysis creatively, not in conformity to any set of rules that could be defined.

## Towards the future

Art can never promise the certainties that science can, even if it is spurious science. The laws of aerodynamics can tell you whether a particular shape of wing will fly or not. The fact that there are no corresponding 'laws of persuasion' is not for want of looking for them, nor to the unhelpfulness of the advertising profession, but to the nature of the human mind and the human decision-making process.

At long last, science may be coming to the aid of the creative department. At the beginning of the 1990s the US government decreed it to be the decade of the mind. One commentator has said that as a result of this we have learnt more about the human brain in the last ten years than we ever knew before. That does not mean we understand it – another expert says it is almost certainly the most complicated subject in the whole of science (Horgan, 1999). Anyone who thinks that another ten years, or even a hundred, of neurobiological research will provide the magic set of levers to pull and push that psychologists have been promising since Walter Dill Scott, is likely to be disappointed. What we are already finding is that the nature of decision-making seems very different from what the hierarchical rational models always assumed. There is no such thing as a 'rational' decision. Decisions are all, ultimately, taken with the emotions. (Bill Bernbach would not have been surprised. Twenty years ago, in one of his last speeches, given to the AAAA (American Association of Advertising Agencies), he said that 'Emotions make you feel. And only feeling leads to action… The intellect, it seems, is just a tool at the service of our interests and instincts'.)

Within our minds we each keep an immensely complicated network of memories, associations, and feelings that influence our decision-making. Many of these are unconscious, not in the deep Freudian sense, but simply in the way that we do not know they are happening and normally never articulate or analyse them. The rational cognitive brain does have a part to play, but this seems to be more in the area of justifying what the emotions want to do (Heath, 2001).

All this suggests that those involved in using the art of influencing other people through communications may learn some useful lessons from psychology, but ultimately the art can never be reduced to rules or principles. We respond to the subtlest of nuances. As advertisers we can do it, as well as we ever can, only because we are people too, and share some of the sensitivities of those we are communicating with. As neuroscience helps to articulate the physical facts behind all these things we have, on the whole, always really known but could never prove, it will perhaps create for the first time an adequate scientific proof that persuasion is indeed, not a science, but an art.

# References

Bernbach, W. (1980) Facts are not enough. Annual meeting of the American Association of Advertising Agencies, White Sulphur Springs, West Virginia, May 14–17.

Gardner, B.B. & Levy, S.J. (1955) The product and the brand. *Harvard Business Review*, March–April, pp. 33–39.

Gunther, J. (1960) *Taken at the Flood: the Story of Albert D Lasker*. Hamish Hamilton, London.

Heath, R. (2001) *The Hidden Power of Advertising: How Low Involvement Processing Influences the Way We Choose Brands*. Admap Publications, Henley-on-Thames.

Hopkins, C. (1923) *Scientific Advertising*. NTC Business Books, Lincolnwood, Illinois.

Horgan, J. (1999) *The Undiscovered Mind*. Weidenfeld and Nicholson, London.

Joyce, T. (1967) What do we know about how advertising works? ESOMAR Seminar, Nordwijk am See: reprinted in Broadbent, S. (1980), *Market Researchers Look at Advertising*, pp. 27–28. ESOMAR, Amsterdam.

Martineau, P. (1957) *Motivation in Advertising*. McGraw Hill, New York.

Mayer, M. (1958) *Madison Avenue USA*. The Bodley Head, London.

Packard, V. (1957) *The Hidden Persuaders*. Longmans, Green & Co, London.

Pollitt, S. (2001) *Pollitt on Planning*. Admap Publications, Henley-on-Thames.

Reeves, R. (1961) *Reality in Advertising*. Alfred A. Knopf, New York.

Schultze, Q.J. (1983) The origins of university-level advertising instruction in the United States, 1900–1917. *Journal of Advertising History* 1, October.

Scott, W.D. (1903) *The Psychology of Advertising*. Small, Maynard & Co, Boston

Starch, D. (1923) *Principles of Advertising*. A.W. Shaw Company, Chicago.

Taylor, F.W. (1911) *The Principles of Scientific Management*. Harper Bros, New York.

# Index